Carmen Turner-Schott's Phoenixes & Angels brilliantly brings the shadows of the 8th and 12th astrological houses out into the light of evolutionary growth. The author is an intuitive empath sharing her knowledge that offers the readers pragmatic paths to transformation colored with empowering insights.
Bernie Ashman, author of *Astrological Games People Play, How to Survive Mercury Retrograde: And Venus & Mars, Too*, and other titles

Phoenixes & Angels

Mastering the Eighth & Twelfth Astrological Houses

Phoenixes & Angels

Mastering the Eighth & Twelfth Astrological Houses

Carmen Turner-Schott,
MSW, LISW

Winchester, UK
Washington, USA

JOHN HUNT PUBLISHING

First published by O-Books, 2023
O-Books is an imprint of John Hunt Publishing Ltd., 3 East St., Alresford,
Hampshire SO24 9EE, UK
office@jhpbooks.com
www.johnhuntpublishing.com
www.o-books.com

For distributor details and how to order please visit the 'Ordering' section on our website.

ISBN: 978 1 80341 080 7
978 1 80341 081 4 (ebook)
Library of Congress Control Number: 2022938082

A CIP catalogue record for this book is available from the British Library.

Design: Matthew Greenfield

UK: Printed and bound by CPI Group (UK) Ltd, Croydon, CR0 4YY
Printed in North America by CPI GPS partners

We operate a distinctive and ethical publishing philosophy in
all areas of our business, from our global network of authors to
production and worldwide distribution.

Contents

About the Author   xiii

Artist   xv

Dedication   xvi

Introduction   1

Part One: Mastering the Eighth House   17

  Chapter One: Transformation and Resilience   19

  Chapter Two: Power   28

  Chapter Three: Childhood Secrets & Deep
    Emotions and Privacy   32

  Chapter Four: Intense Relationships & Sexuality
    and Intimacy   39

  Chapter Five: Karma and Past Lives   45

  Chapter Six: Death, Loss, Endings, Rebirth,
    and Regeneration   50

  Chapter Seven: Healing & Forgiveness   58

  Chapter Eight: Healer Versus Healed   67

  Chapter Nine: Spiritual Gifts and Psychic
    Abilities   70

  Chapter Ten: Depression, Anger, Anxiety,
    and Repression   77

  Chapter Eleven: Other People's Resources,
    Inheritances, and Sacrifice   83

  Chapter Twelve: Trauma and Self-Care   87

  Chapter Thirteen: Planets in the Eighth &
    Transits through the Eighth   99

  Chapter Fourteen: Eighth House Phoenixes'
    Greatest Strengths and Weaknesses   127

  Chapter Fifteen: Eighth House Phoenixes'
    Personal Wisdom   136

Part Two: Mastering the Twelfth House   **147**

Chapter One: Solitude, Retreat, Isolation,
and Seclusion   149

Chapter Two: Psychic Abilities and Mystical
Experiences   152

Chapter Three: Escapism, Detachment, and
Addiction & Secrets and Illusions   158

Chapter Four: Foreign Countries and Large
Animals   167

Chapter Five: Dreaming, Dreamwork, Sleep,
and Rest   175

Chapter Six: Sun & Moon: Karma with Father and
Mother & Developing Boundaries   204

Chapter Seven: Suffering, Empathy, and
Compassion   208

Chapter Eight: Romanticism, Heartbreak, and
Love Lessons   211

Chapter Nine: Invisibility, Secret Enemies,
and Hidden Talents   214

Chapter Ten: Depression, Sadness, and Loneliness
& Spiritual Connection and Cosmic
Consciousness   221

Chapter Eleven: Behind the Scenes: Prisons,
Hospitals, Monasteries, and Government   225

Chapter Twelve: Planets in the Twelfth & Transits
through the Twelfth   227

Chapter Thirteen: Twelfth House Angels'
Personal Wisdom   255

Chapter Fourteen: Twelfth House and Self-Care   258

Conclusion   261

Other Titles by this Author

*Sun Signs, Houses & Healing: Build Resilience and
Transform Your Life through Astrology*
ISBN: 978-0738771304

The Mysteries of the Twelfth Astrological House
ISBN: 978-1-78099-343-0

The Mysteries of the Eighth Astrological House
ISBN: 9781450534505

A Practical Look at the Planets through the Houses
ISBN: 978-1468016246

A Deeper Look at the Sun Signs
ISBN: 1419652176

Astrology From a Christian Perspective

Astrology Awareness: A Compilation of Articles.

About the Author

Photo by Janice Turner

Carmen Turner-Schott, MSW, LISW is a practicing clinical social worker, author, and astrologer with national and international clientele. She graduated from Washington University in St. Louis with a Master of Social Work degree in 1999. She currently works as a Sexual Assault Prevention and Response Program Manager and has worked with victims of trauma for over 25 years.

Carmen began her astrological work at the age of 16, after an experience with a glowing ball of light in her doorway. She began studying religion, psychology, and astrology at that time. She has lectured and presented astrology workshops and eGroups for the Association of Research and Enlightenment (A.R.E.) Edgar Cayce Foundation. She also enjoys teaching a variety of spiritual development classes.

For the past 25 years, Carmen has been researching astrology, transformation, and healing. She founded the Astrological Self Awareness Center in 2005 and later changed the name to Deep Soul Divers Astrology. She has a passion for researching psychological astrology and specializes in the eighth and twelfth astrological houses and their effects on trauma, healing, and resiliency.

She is a published author and her two most recent books are *Sun Signs, Houses & Healing: Build Resilience & Transform Your Life through Astrology* with Llewelyn Publishing and *The Mysteries of the Twelfth Astrological House: Fallen Angels* with John Hunt Publishing, both released in 2022. She has also self-published five astrology books, *The Mysteries of the Eighth Astrological House: Phoenix Rising, A Deeper Look at the Sun Signs, A Practical Look at the Planets through the Houses, Astrology From a Christian Perspective*, and *Astrology Awareness: A Compilation of Articles*.

You can learn more about Carmen and her work by visiting www.8and12houses.com, Facebook Author Page at www.facebook.com/CarmenTurnerSchottWriter/, and at https://www.facebook.com/www.deepsouldiversastrology

Artist Essam Issadi

Uranian Kid is a 16-year-old artist who was born in a small-town west of Algeria. He loves spiritual art, astrology, music, painting and sculpting. His dream is to have a career as an artist.

He reached out to Carmen through her YouTube channel and developed a series of dream images to include in this book. You can contact him at uraniankido@gmail.com for more information on his graphic design ideas.

Dedication

One does not become enlightened by imagining figures of light, but by making the darkness conscious.
– Carl Jung

I want to thank all the eighth and twelfth house people from all over the world who have reached out to me and shared their personal stories of strength, courage, and resiliency. I have spent many years researching both houses and have found common themes. I am extremely grateful to be able to write a book for others that shares the spiritual truths, life lessons, challenges, and strengths that these houses create in our lives. In this book, we will discuss personal life experiences that come with having planets in these two spiritually transforming houses. I coined the term "deep soul divers" to represent individuals who have planets in the eighth and twelfth astrological houses.

Eighth and twelfth house people are special souls who are always seeking deeper meaning in life. They are searching for answers and drawn to the mystical and spiritual side of life. Deep soul divers are lights that shine brightly in the darkness. Other people are drawn to them and they attract others who suffer emotionally, who are lonely, or those who are in pain. They attract people that are wounded and need healing. Sent here to assist others on their spiritual journeys, they are ancient caretakers and servants. They're transformative healers who heal because they have been wounded themselves. They can use that understanding to help others transform their pain. Digging deep down beneath the surface is their gift. Uncovering secrets and problems that need to come to light comes naturally for them.

I was thinking about all the people in my life who I have worked with and many of them had planets in the eighth and twelfth astrological houses. I realized that the one connection that they all had was the fact that they are shining lights for anyone who needs support. They attract people and are natural psychologists capable of helping those in need.

My own eighth and twelfth house stories have played out throughout my entire life, making me the person I am today. In 2014, the planet Uranus began transiting my eighth house. This transit forced me to face hidden parts of myself that I did not realize lived inside me. It reminded me of Harry Potter in the *Deathly Hallows* when he realized he was a horcrux and that a part of the darkness lived inside of him. He realized he had to die and be reborn again out of the ashes. During this time, I struggled with feelings and thoughts that had never surfaced before. Many people with eighth and twelfth house planets experience these emotional changes, transformations and rebirths.

Embracing our shadow, similar to Carl Jung's archetype theory of personality, is eighth and twelfth house territory. Individuals with planets in the eighth and twelfth houses spend a lot of time trying to understand themselves and others better while searching for the meaning of life. They are tested more than other people. Many have to be reborn several times throughout their lives through challenging experiences. It is their destiny to live through experiences that most people can never understand. They are resilient and capable of surviving the most traumatic experiences. Deep soul divers use their wisdom to guide others on their healing journeys.

Introduction

Knowing your own darkness is the best method for dealing with the darknesses of other people.
– Carl Jung

Eighth and Twelfth House People

When I refer to others as eighth and twelfth house people it relates to individuals who have planets placed in the eighth and twelfth houses in their astrological birth chart. It can also represent someone who has an abundance of Scorpio and Pisces energy. The eighth house is ruled by the sign Scorpio and its planetary ruler is Pluto. The twelfth house is ruled by the sign Pisces and Neptune is the planetary ruler. Pluto energy is associated with issues such as power, death, rebirth, control, healing, transformation, secrets, regeneration, psychic abilities, and powerful change. The planet Neptune's energy involves spirituality, escapism, suffering, illusion, addiction, romanticism, artistic abilities, and intuition.

Both houses have been the focus of my research since 1998. Having a *stellium* in either of these two transforming houses means there are three or more planets in a single house. When this happens, it intensifies the eighth or twelfth house energy. I believe that even having just one planet placed in either of these houses is extremely important.

When planets transit either of these houses, the energy will be valuable, powerful, and life changing. Everyone at some time in their life will have planets transit through these houses and will benefit by learning more about them. Having planets placed in these two houses in the birth chart is special and the individual will have an important mission. Knowing the entire birth chart is important in understanding your full personality, but the purpose of this book is to focus on issues related to these

1

specific houses. There are many positive lessons that these two houses create, even though having planets in these houses are traditionally known to bring difficulties. In this book, I am going to focus on the strengths of both houses and provide tips to overcome the more challenging energies.

Throughout this book, I will share stories from clients who shared their personal experiences, observations, and lessons in order to help others. Several topics will be discussed throughout the chapters. I will share examples of spiritual experiences and special abilities that many people with planets in these houses naturally possess. I hope there is something that you can find helpful in your astrological journey.

The Nautilus Shell

Symbol of Eighth & Twelfth House People

There is no coming to consciousness without pain.
– Carl Jung

Forever Changed, Transformed and Reborn

In 2015, while I was living in Germany, I went to bed one night and had the most vivid dream. This dream came at a time in my life where I had felt lonely, stressed, and depressed. I was searching to find myself again, to find the person that I used to be. Looking back at my life I felt very different than how I felt in the past. I wanted to feel like my old self again. It was like a part of me died, and a part of me was gone forever, and I was trying to accept the new me.

During this time in my life, I was working with sexual assault victims as a victim advocate. I witnessed the trauma, pain, and betrayal they had experienced. I realized how much I had seen and gone through as a social worker in such a short amount of time. Personally, and professionally, I felt forever changed. The person that I was in the past did not exist anymore. I had to get used to this new version of me, the new and improved Carmen.

It was a difficult time in my life, and I could not even put into words what I experienced. The transformations were deep and beyond words. I did not even have the energy at that time to try to explain what I was going through to anyone. I was regenerated out of the ashes and rose up like a phoenix. I had to take baby steps towards getting used to these new emotions and personality traits. I had to learn to accept myself. When you experience transformation, you must let go of the past fully and come to terms with new emotional depths.

This transformation of my personality happened when the planet Uranus began transiting my eighth house in the sign of Aries. Not only was it transiting the house of death, transformation, and rebirth, but it was also hitting my natal planets which sat in the eighth house. It was influencing my Moon, Jupiter, and Chiron. This transit was bringing up many hidden wounds from my unconscious to heal once and for all.

Important Nautilus Dream

One night I went to sleep and, in my dream, I saw the beautiful ocean. The deep blue ocean was calling me. Standing on the bank of the ocean I saw a man standing there with a boat. My friend Emma was there with me. We got on the boat together. We were searching for fossils. The man in the boat took us far out into the beautiful turquoise blue water. He stopped the boat out in the middle of the ocean. I looked to the left and saw an embankment of sand. We swam over to explore and there were white- and crème-colored stones lying everywhere. Rummaging through the rocks, and stones, I kept looking for something special.

Suddenly, I saw something and I picked up a stone with the

shape of a spiral on it. A fossil was imprinted on it and it had an amazing design. I had never seen this shape before. I had no idea what it meant but I knew it was special. I held the stone-shaped design in my hand with wonder. I knew it was a message for me. I swam back to the boat with Emma and we traveled back to the shore. Immediately after we returned, I woke up.

I wrote this dream down immediately. I was intrigued and knew this dream was important. I began to research fossils online but was not sure what to search for. I started messaging Emma and told her about my dream. I asked her what she thought it meant. She immediately wrote back and sent me a picture. As soon as I opened her message I saw the picture—I was shocked. It was the same shape I held in my hand in the dream. Emma told me it was a Nautilus. I had never heard of that before so I started researching and was amazed by what I found. The Nautilus fossil is associated with sacred geometry. Sacred geometry involves the belief that symbolic and sacred meanings are associated with certain geometric shapes. It is associated with the belief that God is the great geometer of the world. The geometry used in the design of the nautilus shell is used to construct pyramids, temples, churches, altars, and mosques.

According to Stephen Skinner, the study of sacred geometry has been found in nature and mathematical principles. The most well-known form of this is the Nautilus shell as it grows at a constant rate and its shell forms a logarithmic spiral when it can grow without changing shape. The shell itself is linked to the Golden Ratio and associated with the Fibonacci sequence. It contains deep mathematical calculations showing the connection of everything in nature and within our physical body.

After reading about the Nautilus shell, I purchased a few stones and earrings. I was fascinated by this fossil. I realized that the Nautilus was similar to individuals who have planets in the eighth and twelfth houses. Deep soul divers are forever changed inside their physical form emotionally, spiritually, psychologically, and mentally just like the Nautilus. They have to adapt constantly to their environment until they outgrow their home. According to Wikipedia, the nautilus has survived relatively unchanged for millions of years and is considered a "living fossil".

Nautiluses are old souls with ancient wisdom just like people with eighth and twelfth house planets. All the experiences they go through in their lives, ones that are painful, intense, and transforming, change them inside forever. They are survivors just like the ancient Nautilus. Nothing can prevent them from surviving because they are born with an inborn resilience to overcome obstacles that impact their environment and life.

I chose to write about the Nautilus because it fits two important symbolic meanings. It symbolizes that we constantly change and grow inside as eighth and twelfth house people. Secondly, it relates to the deep soul diver term. The word Nautilus is a Greek word meaning "sailor" (Wikipedia). The Nautilus is a deep soul diver who lives deep within the ocean (which represents emotions and spirit) and experiences its life in deep waters.

These creatures are almost extinct and are very rare. They are special, just like people with eighth and twelfth house planets. The spiritual world is something that they are connected to as they have been in existence for millions of years. With a strong outer shell that protects them, it helps them adapt to the ever-changing environment. Every time I connected with someone and felt that they were like me, I found out that they had planets in the eighth or twelfth houses. They are seeking to find out the truth about why they are here and what their soul has come to earth to learn. They share a comrade with each other and can relate because of similar experiences.

Phoenixes

Eighth House People

Meditating on the Phoenix, I saw what I had to go through to stop using drugs and alcohol. I had to leave my old self behind and that included all of the people I associated with. The bird rising up and looking straight ahead with the determination of one who knows what the alternative is. Taking the chance of moving into something new and scary. Not knowing if I would make it, or even like the new me, but knowing there was no going back.
– Female, California

When planets are placed in the eighth house the energy and life situations experienced are intense, deep, and life changing. Eighth house people are forced to experience change. The story of the phoenix in ancient mythology is an interesting tale. The phoenix is known to possess great strength and the power to overcome death. This bird destroys itself through fire and turns to ashes only to be reborn into a completely new bird. This symbolizes the process of rebirth, regeneration, and transformation which are all related to the eighth house.

As phoenixes, people with planets in the eighth house rise from the ashes after difficult life situations. Throughout their lives many eighth house people experience emotional deaths where they feel like the person they were before had completely been changed. When they look in the mirror, they don't even recognize themselves anymore because they feel and think differently. They have a whole new way of experiencing life. It can be a painful process when they are forced to go through these transformations. Sometimes holding onto the past, not forgiving, and refusing to let go of outdated emotions is what triggers these rebirths.

Eighth house phoenixes self-transform naturally after challenging experiences and are beacons of healing. The pain, heartache, and difficulties they experience turn into strengths that can be used to assist others. The strengths they develop come from their ability to release the old and regenerate themselves. Eighth house people are resilient because they keep moving forward after tragedy and crisis. They are known to adapt to emotional pain and face it head-on by discipline, drive, forgetting, forgiving, dying, and adapting into a stronger and wiser person.

Everyone has something in their astrology chart that can be difficult. Traditionally the eighth house has always been considered a tragic area of life but there have been a lot of misunderstanding and fears surrounding this house. The truth is everything that is considered taboo in our society falls into the eighth house. Sex and death to name a few. Eighth house planets can bring trauma into our lives, karmic lessons, and betrayal but the goal of these placements is to create growth. Phoenixes are beacons of light and are full of strength and hope. Destined to face loss, betrayal, and wounding is part of their journey. These painful experiences from childhood, past relationships, betrayal, and death of loved ones have to be overcome and processed.

The strengths they develop come from their ability to let go and release old energy. The energy of Pluto assists eighth house people in moving forward. They are the world's healers, therapists, counselors, and wise teachers.

Angels

Twelfth House People

Ever since I was a child, I felt different from other people. I was obsessed with angels and collected angel figurines throughout childhood and into my teenage years. I knew something was watching over me, protecting me, like an unseen force. I felt like I was an alien or adopted because I was psychic and would dream things that would happen.
– Female, California

When planets are placed in the twelfth house the experiences you have are mystical, spiritual, unexplained, and secretive. The twelfth house is where you search to find your soul and your connection to spirit. The meaning of life and your soul's purpose can be found in this house. Diving down into the deep waters of your soul and connecting with others and emerging stronger than ever before is the mission of angels.

Through experiencing suffering and feeling emotional pain, you realize your connection to everyone and everything. There is a sense of oneness that is felt and an ability to serve others on a deeper level. Dreams, fantasy, fairy tales, and illusions make the twelfth house an imaginative dream world where anything is possible. Amazing artistic and musical abilities can manifest when planets are in the twelfth.

Experiencing the unexplained is something that comes naturally for people with planets here. Spiritual and psychic abilities help twelfth house people feel a sense of purpose. It is true that they have a special mission. A mission to overcome and conquer overwhelming feelings of escaping and detaching from this world. Twelfth house people often feel different from others and like they are from another world. Some feel a sense of not belonging to the family they are born in. Sensitive and empathic they feel the pain that surrounds them. They feel separate but want to belong.

Compassionate and kind, they often feel a desire to help everyone. Twelfth house people are God's messengers on earth. I refer to them as angels. Twelfth house people share with me that they don't feel human. Even from a young age, many individuals with twelfth house planets feel they are different from normal people. They are extremely kind, naïve, and intuitive. They believe that other people are kind like them but they find out that is not the case. Feelings get hurt easily and the harshness of this world shocks them. Some astrologers believe that having the Sun in the twelfth house shows an old soul and that this could be their last lifetime. Serving others and sacrificing oneself to heal others comes naturally. Angels who fell to earth to support and uplift the lives of others, they are destined to come out of the mist and be seen. Walking in two worlds, with one foot in the spiritual and one in reality helps them find peace. They are born with many blessings such as spiritual gifts, psychic abilities, artistic talents, creativity, and the ability to listen to others. Their connection and oneness with a higher power is a blessing and their greatest gift.

The Eighth House

Phoenix Energy
Ruled by Scorpio & Planetary Ruler Pluto
Lessons: Healing, Forgiveness, Letting Go, Psychological Insight

The greatest psychological depths are found when planets are placed in the eighth astrological house. No wonder this house is full of strength and intensity, it's ruled by the sign Scorpio. Death, sexuality and all darker areas of life reside here. This is the house that makes people feel uncomfortable. The house where we experience death, loss, endings, trauma, betrayal, sexual intimacy, secrets, inheritances, benefits through other people's resources, emotional pain, and karmic wounds. It is a place where we find solutions and answers to life's most tragic problems. Planets here are karmic learning tools destined to create healing, growth, and transformation in our lives. Even when life knocks them down, they always fight hard to get back up again. Strength is developed through sacrifice and focusing on others' needs. Learning how to forgive and let go of the past is an eighth house lesson. Developing psychological insight through profound experiences and greater self-awareness is eighth house territory.

Some of the key areas the eighth house is associated with are listed below for easy reference.

1. Death, Endings, and Loss
   - Symbolic death of the self
   - Fascination with physical death
   - Interest in the afterlife, soul, astral realm, ghosts, and spirits
   - Deep understanding of death through loss of a loved one
   - Transformation through emotional changes, beliefs, and behaviors

2. Rebirth, Transformation, and Regeneration
   - Victimization & Traumatic experiences
   - Suffering
   - Depression and loneliness
   - Forgiveness and understanding
   - Letting go and releasing things
   - Transformation of the self
   - Embracing change

3.   Healing Abilities
   - Sensitivity to the environment and sensing energy
   - Ability to feel and sense people's pain
   - Reiki and Pranic healing
   - Massage therapy, reflexology, healing touch, and acupuncture
   - Counseling and helping those that need deep healing

4.   Psychic Abilities
   - Intuition
   - Clairsentience, clairaudience, and clairvoyance
   - Astral experiences
   - Dreams
   - Awareness of spirits, angels, and ghosts
   - Higher levels of consciousness
   - Channeling and automatic writing

5.   Repression and Secrets
   - Holding on to the past
   - Denying our pain
   - Inability to feel emotions
   - Anger and irritability
   - Depression, anxiety, and destructive behaviors
   - Health problems, sexual dysfunction, and illnesses
   - Sexual abuse issues, unhealed trauma
   - Intimacy concerns and trust issues

6.   Other People's Resources and Inheritances
   - Inheritances (material and emotional)
   - Spouse's finances and shared resources
   - Land, property, and possessions
   - Material things given to you from others
   - Managing other people's money, stocks, finances, wills, and estates

7. Sacrifice
   - Learning to let go of material things, and emotions such as guilt, regret, and anger
   - Paying a price to help others
   - Letting go or releasing something that we truly desire
   - Embracing difficult changes
   - Focusing on others' wants and needs above our own

The Twelfth House

Angel Energy
Ruled by Pisces & Planetary Ruler Neptune
Lessons: Spiritual Connection, Service to Others, Developing Boundaries, Staying Grounded

The twelfth house is the most mystical, mysterious and spiritual house in the astrological chart. When planets are placed in the twelfth we experience unexplained psychic experiences, spiritual connections and a strong secretive nature. The twelfth house is where we search to find ourselves and a connection to God. Seeking the meaning of life and finding a soul mission is the destiny that has to be mastered in this house. Learning to emerge emotionally stronger by developing boundaries is part of their purpose.

The key issues related to the twelfth house are cosmic consciousness, escapism, service to others, mystical experiences, isolation, addiction, and compassion. Through experiencing suffering and feeling the emotional pain of others, twelfth house people realize they are meant to lessen the pain of others. They can use their intuitive abilities to prepare for future events. Sometimes it's like there are angels watching over them protecting them from harm, especially when Jupiter is placed here.

Dreams, fairy tales, and illusions make the twelfth house an imaginative, creative, artsy world where anything is possible.

Experiencing the unexplained is a special gift for people with planets here and restores their faith in a higher power. They indeed have a special mission, a mission of service.

Overcoming overwhelming feelings of wanting to escape from the practical world can be a challenge so they need to learn to stay grounded. Finding a connection to something larger than themselves brings comfort and stability. Sensitive and empathic, they absorb other people's thoughts, feelings, and emotions. Compassionate and kind, they always have a desire to help others. Twelfth house people are God's messengers here on earth.

The key areas the twelfth house is associated with are listed below for easy reference.

1. Escapism and Detachment
    - Sensitivity to the environment
    - Need for isolation, quiet time, rest, and alone time
    - Need for seclusion from the outside world
    - Avoidance of people and withdrawal from everyday life
    - Meditation brings comfort
    - Sleeping and dreaming

2. Psychic Abilities and Mystical Experiences
    - Déjà vu experiences
    - Clairvoyance, dreams, clairaudience, and clairsentience
    - Out of body experiences, near death experiences, angel visitations, seeing ghosts
    - Past life memories
    - Intuition and inner knowing
    - Sensitivity to others; feeling other people's pain, and heightened empathy

3. Confinement, Hospitals, Prisons, Monasteries, and Temples
   - Isolation through a spiritual path or religious organization
   - Dedicated life of prayer, meditation, and spirituality
   - Withdrawal from normal society
   - Hidden secrets and behind the scenes identity
   - Becoming a priest, rabbi, monk, or nun
   - Mental illness hospitalizations, health problems, and unforeseen illnesses

4. Seclusion, Privacy, and Withdrawal
   - Hiding true feelings from self and others
   - Secret love affairs and heartache
   - Attraction to individuals who are not "free or healthy"
   - Hiding one's true nature and personality from others
   - Needing alone time and solitude
   - Needing peaceful surroundings

5. Hidden Enemies
   - Fake friends and acquaintances
   - Trusting people too easily
   - Betrayal
   - Being your own worst enemy
   - Being taken advantage of

6. Secrets
   - Those things kept hidden from you or others
   - Family, friends, and lovers' secrets
   - Illusion and delusion to practical reality
   - Seeing things with rose-colored glasses

7. Service to Others
   - Attracting people with problems and those who need

help
- Deep desire to serve others through charity work, spiritual work, and counseling
- Self-sacrificing behavior
- Need to develop boundaries to protect themselves
- Taking on other people's energy, pain, and problems
- Confidant, counselor, therapist, and helper

8. Addiction, Alcoholism, Drug Use, and Codependency
    - Potential for addictive behaviors
    - Susceptibility to alcoholism, or drug addiction through escapist behaviors
    - Food addiction, love addiction, and work addiction
    - Seeking comfort and numbing oneself through substances
    - Addiction to withdrawing or escaping daily responsibilities

9. Spiritual Connection, Subconscious, Family Karma, and Spiritual Learning
    - Finding a spiritual path
    - Meditation and breathing techniques
    - Studying different spiritual disciplines
    - Focus on a soul mission and special purpose
    - Karma, past lives, and reincarnation
    - Suffering, loss, and feeling invisible

Part One

Mastering the Eighth House

Everything can be taken from a man but one thing: the last of the human freedoms—to choose one's attitude in any given set of circumstances, to choose one's own way.
– Viktor E. Frankl

Chapter One

Transformation and Resilience

You have to die a few times before you can really live.
– Charles Bukowski

People with eighth house planets transform into an entirely new person just like a caterpillar that turns into a beautiful butterfly. Their lives have a special journey and they often experience metamorphosis. Absorbing all the energy around them including positive and negative experiences makes them have a need to withdraw, hide away, and turn inward inside a special cocoon.

When they are inside this cocoon they die. A part of their personality is forever changed. This change is not a physical death, it's an energetic, psychological, emotional, and physical transformation. After the passage of time and deep contemplation on life lessons, they have learned to transform. Beautiful inside and out, they are reborn with an entirely new body, mind, and spirit. The eighth house person survives. Their survival is a miracle and no matter what happens to them, eighth house people always overcome painful experiences. They are resilient souls who use change to ignite growth and resurrection of the self.

We all know the feeling that we experience when we see a beautiful butterfly fluttering around. It's almost like magic to observe butterflies in nature because they look so delicate, yet so strong at the same time. Their beautiful colors and amazing wings are breathtaking. Butterflies are a strong symbol of change, transformation, renewal and rebirth. The journey of a butterfly is very similar to the journey of eighth house people.

Emotional Trauma, Wounds & Forgiveness

The truth is that butterflies did not start out beautiful and many did not feel strong. Just like many eighth house people, they withdraw from the world into their cold, crusty cocoon to help protect themselves. They call this period of transformation the Chrysalis period. Like butterflies, eighth house people hibernate and hide in order to heal. When eighth house people feel hurt, wounded or betrayed, they often are changed on a deeper level. Experiencing emotional trauma such as sexual betrayal is a common experience for people with planets placed in the eighth house. Their wounds can be both physical, psychological, and emotional.

After talking to many clients who have experienced trauma, they often share with me strong desires to be alone to withdraw within themselves to find strength. This hiatus and time in a self-imposed cocoon represented a precious time for them to ignite regeneration. It is during these times of rest, that their wounds begin to heal, and their scars start to fade away. With each passing day and with the passage of time, eighth house people find they can begin to forgive others and themselves. Forgiveness does not miraculously occur overnight and sometimes they take two steps forward and 10 steps back. I promise they will emerge more resilient from the cocoon after they have changed their emotional pain, negative thoughts, beliefs, wounded bodies, and broken hearts. They will emerge. They will be reborn. They will be renewed.

Eighth House Butterflies

It takes patience and a safe place to be alone for eighth house people to benefit from this transformative energy. If they take time to enjoy being away from the world and focus on healing themselves then they will experience growth.

Several years ago, someone I counseled gave me a small gift at our final session together. I opened the package and it was a framed photo of a butterfly. This client shared with me that they felt like a brand-new person after going through alcohol abuse counseling and they wanted to give me a photo of a butterfly that they had photographed. I kept this in my professional office for many years as a reminder of how counseling transforms and changes us. It also symbolized all the progress, growth, and healing that this client had accomplished.

One spring, I was sitting outside on my deck to get some fresh air in my garden and saw a cocoon of a caterpillar attached to one of the plants. It was not beautiful and looked almost alien. I could see the butterfly sleeping inside the crusty cocoon. I thought to myself, "How amazing it was that this living thing inside there will transform soon into a beautiful butterfly." A few months later, I went outside and this amazing butterfly flew right up to me and landed on my arm. I smiled, knowing that the dark time in my life was going to come to an end. I had struggled long enough in my cocoon of healing. I had lost people that I loved and death showed up on my front doorstep. I never truly knew how to talk about it with those closest to me, so I didn't. I just pushed forward in life, working, doing my daily routine but never truly healed my own wounds. Around this same time, my neighbor told me that she had a birthday gift for me. She came over and gave me a box to open, and she said to hold it out away from my face. I opened the box and there was a beautiful newborn butterfly. She said, "She was just born," and told me to hold out my finger. The gorgeous butterfly walked onto my finger and stayed with me.

I had her take a photo because I was amazed and then right before my eyes this newly changed butterfly flew for the first time and used its new wings. I decided that day, I was going to let go of things from the past that were holding me back from moving forward with my healing journey. Releasing painful thoughts, emotions, and memories once and for all was my new goal.

Letting Go & Self-Reliance

The feeling of freedom that comes once we burst out of our cocoon is truly inspiring and provides us with hope. Often the most difficult task for people with planets in the eighth house is to embrace true forgiveness. We must forgive others for the hurt we perceive they have caused us. Holding onto anger, rage, sadness, disappointment, and negative emotions only hurt us. We forgive others for ourselves. Forgiving others does not mean that something bad did not happen, or that others never wronged us. We forgive others because it is what helps us heal. There is a special mission associated with the eighth house and it is releasing things that no longer serve our growth. This can be challenging and take time to master.

Strength to Emerge on Our Own

There is a relevant story about the butterfly during the chrysalis period. A Guru asked a boy not to help a butterfly when it was trying to break free from the chrysalis. The boy did not listen to the advice of watching the butterfly struggle on its own. He helped the butterfly when it was struggling to poke out of the cocoon. He watched how painful it was for the butterfly and he could not bear to watch it struggle. The butterfly died, and the Guru told the boy that the butterfly needed to struggle so that its wings would grow strong enough to fly once it was hatched. The moral of the story is that the butterfly is destined to emerge on its own because if it doesn't, it won't be strong enough to fly with its new wings.

We can see how this relates to the feelings that many eighth house people experience. Eighth house people often feel that no one is around for them when they need them the most. Clients have shared with me that they believe they have to do things by themselves, and can only depend on themselves for strength and support. Once they emerge from their cocoon, they realize that the darkest times are now behind them. They are ready to break free. They are forever changed, healed, and reinvigorated.

Journeys & Cycles

We all go through journeys and cycles in our lives. Eighth house people are always experiencing these cycles of rebirth. The energy of the eighth house forces people to adapt to the environment and shed their skin, withdraw and reemerge. Sometimes eighth house people feel sad and mourn their old personality. Growth can be painful and uncomfortable. We often resist it. Once eighth house people allow themselves to burst free from the cocoon, they are truly able to help others do the same. Eighth house people are like transformed butterflies. They lead the way in helping others heal their wounds because they have mastered how to do this on their own.

Wounded Healers

Eighth house people can't hide forever. They tend to repress their sadness, anger, depression, anxiety, and negative feelings. They are known to dwell on these negative emotions because they feel things so deeply. Eighth house people struggle to communicate how they feel. It is easier for them to write down their thoughts versus communicating them verbally. They need to come out of the shadows and allow their beauty to be seen and felt by other people. They must accept newness and the new version of themselves.

Embracing change, whether that change is internal or external is crucial for healing and morphing into an enchanting butterfly. They must heal their own wounds in order to help others heal. They are true healers in this world, attracting others who have similar pain. Only after they learn how to accept these periods of metamorphosis, renewal, and change can they begin to live their special mission as a wounded healer.

The Resilient Eighth House

For many years, I have helped clients from all over the world who have planets in the eighth house. The one thing that they all have in common is that each of them experienced some type of loss, trauma, betrayal, or emotional wound. Most people do not recognize the strength that eighth house people have and would never even know about the sacrifices these individuals have made throughout their lives. The secrets eighth house people keep are often deep, dark, taboo, and mysterious. Even those closest to them are often unaware of the hidden inner intensity that people with planets in this house possess. They are private and dislike sharing the painful experiences that they lived through. Preferring to take care of things on their own, they tend to suffer in silence.

Survival Skills

Eighth house people rise from the ashes healing from things that most normal people would struggle to survive through. Most people would give up, retreat, and struggle to recover. Eighth house people might get knocked down, but they always get back up again. When they do, they bounce back even stronger. Eighth house people are born with survival skills. They learn to depend on themselves from an early age. The ability to heal, regenerate, and transform within creates resiliency, and with time they can truly forgive others although they never forget.

Overcoming Tragedy

Imagine that someone close to you who you loved more than anyone betrays and abandons you unexpectedly. What would you do? Imagine that your only child dies in a tragic car accident. What would you do? Imagine that your closest friend ends their life by suicide. What would you do? Imagine that someone you trusted took advantage of your love and you felt used, traumatized, and abused because you trusted that person. How would you move forward? How do you heal from something devastating? It's called resiliency.

Wounded Healers

All eighth house people are naturally resilient. Resiliency means you are capable of withstanding shock without permanent damage and tend to recover from or adjust easily from misfortune or change (Webster's Dictionary). Eighth house people develop resilience from overcoming difficult life experiences. They may hit rock bottom, suffer from depression, and struggle to get out of bed each day. These feelings might last for days, months, or years, and then out of the blue, a voice inside tells them to, "Get up."

That voice within is the sound of resiliency. That voice tells them they can overcome anything and that it's time to rise again. They must rise above the pain because the world depends on them. They must stand up, dust off all the pain, and walk away from it. They are born to be true healers, helping those who are wounded and lost. That's why people with planets in the eighth house are often called the "wounded healers".

Phoenixes

Eighth house people are meant to rise like a Phoenix out of the ashes. They must let the past die to release past hurts and trauma. They are meant to let go, destined to become beacons of hope for those who are hopeless. Eighth house people are meant to be a listening ear for those who have sad stories to tell. They are destined to be there for someone who needs a good friend and a good hug in their greatest moment of need. They are meant to support others who are struggling. Born with extreme empathy for those who suffer, they know what it feels like. The eighth house is not just the house of death and transformation. It's the house of resiliency. A place where you overcome tragedy and grow stronger as a person.

Below is a cheat sheet that shows planets in the eighth and how they encourage resiliency. You find resilience from changing and transforming the following:

Sun in the Eighth – Your main identity, appearance, and personality.

Moon in the Eighth – Your inner emotions, feelings, and need to nurture others.

Mercury in the Eighth – Your communication, thoughts, ideas, and beliefs.

Venus in the Eighth – Your need for peace, harmony, love, and relationships.

Mars in the Eighth – Your drive to succeed, aggression, anger, and passion.

Jupiter in the Eighth – Your positive energy, generosity, natural abundance, and optimism.

Saturn in the Eighth – Your responsibilities, burdens, karmic debts, and the past.

Uranus in the Eighth – Your ability to adapt to change and unexpected loss.

Neptune in the Eighth – Your ability to see things clearly, embrace suffering, and find intimacy.

Pluto in the Eighth – Your ability to accept death, loss, trauma, and forgiveness.

Chiron in the Eighth – Your emotional wounds, healing, painful experiences, and grief.

Chapter Two

Power

People often seem uncomfortable around me but end up telling me all their problems.
– C.J.

Eighth house people are powerful. What does it mean to be powerful? It is an ability to influence other people and create change. Eighth house people are born with power even if they do not recognize it. It can take many years before they realize how powerful they are. It can take several painful experiences where they feel their power is taken away from them before they embrace the power they are destined to have. Other people will perceive them as strong and sometimes unapproachable. People either love eighth house people or they fear them. The culprit for these interactions with others is the planet Pluto which intensifies power. Having planets in the eighth will enhance your power. I believe each planet in the eighth influences how you use your power and how others want to take power from you. People will want to be friends with you or pretend to be so they can benefit from your energy. Sometimes you might wonder why certain people use your name at work and talk about you like they are aligned with you. They want others to believe that you are close to them. This is a common example eighth house people share with me. Sometimes they feel used by others but they have an ability to see through people to their true motives.

For example, if the Sun is in the eighth, your personality and identity is powerful. You have a powerful magnetic energy when you walk into a room. When people first meet you there is a mysterious, deep, strong presence that speaks without you even having to say a word. Your power comes from your ability to shine a flashlight on the darker aspects of life. This involves the secrets people keep. Deep, penetrative eyes that show wisdom attracts others into your space. Healing energy radiates from your aura attracting people with pain. You might not even be aware of how powerful your personality can be. The Moon in the eighth will express power by manipulating emotions and feelings. Affecting the environment by controlling the flow of expression is a powerful ability. A heightened intuition, empathy, and perception of the emotional undercurrents in the environment is a powerful gift. Other people's hidden, private, and secretive emotions will be exposed when they are in your presence. You make other people feel things they typically avoid feeling. People will share their problems with you naturally but then wonder why they did so. Sometimes they will feel uncomfortable because you make them feel vulnerable.

When Mercury is in the eighth house, power can be expressed through communication and spreading of knowledge. You could be an influential speaker, presenter, or teacher. When you talk people listen because your words have depth, insight, and wisdom. There might be an ability to control other people's minds or read people's thoughts. Mars in the eighth gives a strong sexual appeal. Other people will sense your powerful drive and competitive nature. Very few people will be able to keep up with your stamina. Hidden anger can bubble under the surface but you are good at repressing it. You can use anger in positive ways to overcome many obstacles. The person with Venus in the eighth house will express power through expressing love and affection. They are seen as magnetic and attractive. You have a powerful ability to make things more beautiful and bring peace to your surroundings. Powerful artistic abilities are common where you can touch deep emotional currents creating powerful emotions in others.

Jupiter in the eighth gives the power of generosity and

kindness. Other people feel your powerful forgiving nature and are drawn to you like moths to a flame. Strong powerful healers, other people want to be in your presence to feel your glow. This is a powerful position of Jupiter that transforms pain and increases healing abilities. Saturn sitting in the eighth will give the power of wisdom, patience, and strength. Even if you don't feel this way about yourself, others will perceive you as practical and reliable. Super responsible, you are known to go without things to help your family survive financially. You can resist temptation and have an immense ability to control your own emotions. Controlling others in subtle ways is your secret power. Sometimes other people do not even realize what is happening to them and they will follow your orders willingly. Your energy demands respect.

When Neptune is placed in the eighth house you have the power of deception. This means you can make other people see things the way you want them to. Imaginative, creative, with an ability to charm, you sweep others up into your energetic web. Others can't seem to figure you out and this mysterious energy attracts those who are spiritual or seeking help. Compassion exudes from your aura and other people see you as illusive. They are attracted to you because they feel there is something hidden, secretive, and special about you. Uranus in the eighth house has the power of shocking people into changing their ways. Eccentric and restless, you have the power to make other people feel unsettled. They can't ever really figure out what you are feeling or who you really are because you appear changeable and unsteady. Your power to force change on your environment and on those who are stuck in a rut is powerful.

Pluto in the eighth house finds itself comfortable in its natural home. Power is intensified by a need for controlling the emotions. Being able to keep secrets is your power. Other people also like to share their secrets with you and almost feel forced to do so. People with Pluto here listen and therefore gather information from everyone without revealing much about themselves. Healing abilities are strong with Pluto in the eighth, and deep psychological discussions help you feel connected to others. With a dislike for fakeness and superficiality, you will cut people off who don't resonate with your energy. Chiron is not a planet, but as an asteroid, it brings a powerful healing quality. Your power comes through experiencing pain, betrayal, loss, and sacrifice because you are a wounded healer. Other people respect your life experience as you radiate depth and inner strength. Other people sense your healing energy. You might not realize how your presence impacts the lives of others in positive ways. They know that you will understand their pain and they trust your guidance. Helping others heal is the key to healing yourself.

Using power and becoming more comfortable with expressing your power brings experience. It makes eighth house people natural leaders that others want to follow. People with power can change the world in positive ways. Eighth house people can utilize their power to attain their goals and dreams. Power brings success in many endeavors and enhances eighth house people's confidence in themselves.

Chapter Three

Childhood Secrets & Deep Emotions and Privacy

Three things cannot long stay hidden: the sun, the moon and the truth.
– Buddha

Childhood Secrets

When I was a child, I never knew that I was adopted but found out unexpectedly.
– A.J.

Keeping secrets comes naturally for eighth house people. Secrets are something that is associated with the astrological sign Scorpio. Being private, hiding things about your family and relatives helps you feel in control. Many people with eighth house planets do not do this on purpose. It is part of their inner nature and the deeper personality they are born with. There is a tendency to want to withdraw from sharing too much of themselves and this behavior often starts in childhood. They dislike being vulnerable and being perceived as a burden to others. They especially hate being seen as weak or incapable of taking care of themselves. They often experience relationships where trust is broken early in life and this impacts them emotionally. To avoid getting hurt, they guard their true thoughts and emotions. Eighth house people have a difficult time remembering things that happened in their childhood. Many have repressed childhood memories that they have buried deep within. Family and relatives often hide things from them when they are children. Other people's secrets can also cause embarrassment and trauma.

They are perceptive and become aware that people are pretending or hiding the truth from them. They can sense emotions, thoughts, and read body language. They can see through and figure out who is lying to them. They have an antenna that notices lies, and once they do, they want to dig to find out more. Eighth house secrets are unique because they are deep, intense, taboo, and embarrassing. Eighth house people were often lied to as children and this truth can manifest in different ways depending on which planets are placed in the eighth house.

Childhood secrets are always exposed. Eighth house people eventually find out what others are trying to hide. They naturally call out secrets around them and it's like opening Pandora's box and everything hidden in the dark is brought to light. Whatever is hidden in the closet we can be sure the eighth house person will seek and expose it. They want to know and understand all the secretive energy that surrounds them.

I remember when I found out that my father's oldest brother was killed by a drunk driver when he was 16 years old. No one ever told me about this until I saw pictures and asked who the boy was in the family photo. It was something my father never shared with me, mainly because it was probably a very painful experience. When doing some research on ancestry with my daughter for her school project I found out some more secrets. My great-grandmother had given birth to a baby who soon died after a few weeks. I did not know about this or that she had her own tombstone until my daughter's project. She had a website where she could look up where people were buried. I learned something new about my family and how secrets always surround us even if we don't realize it. The other thing I realized is that all secrets are eventually revealed to eighth house people if they investigate a little bit.

Some common childhood secrets eighth house people have shared with me are:

- Childhood abuse
- Addiction of a parent
- Some type of trauma
- Unexpected loss
- Death of a loved one
- Psychic abilities and unexplained experiences
- Divorce of parents and secrets about parents
- Secrets about the family (secret adoption, parental paternity)

Secrets are not always negative. Sometimes they are simply other people's secrets and they want them to stay hidden to protect the eighth house person. They often find out the truth concerning family secrets when they are older. When planets are placed in the eighth house the energy is known to make you want to shine a flashlight on all things that are repressed and force them to the surface. When the water is murky you have a way of sifting through the darkness to bring something special to the surface. You always find out what is hidden. Breaking free from painful secrets makes you stronger.

This reminds me of being a child myself and hiding under the covers. You pull the sheet up to hide, but you are not really hiding because anyone can see you are hiding there under the covers. Then you throw the sheet up to peek out and can see everything. Then you hide under the sheet again. Secrets in the eighth house are known, felt, or recognized. Unlike twelfth house secrets that are completely unknown to the person, you will eventually know the truth with eighth house energy. Eighth house people need to heal feelings such as anger, depression, anxiety, and the sadness they experienced as children. Letting go and moving forward from the past will help them forgive, release unpleasant emotions, and focus on the future. They need to remember that everything that happens to them is for spiritual growth. Eighth house people chose a special path this lifetime. They are not being punished by the universe and they need to remember that. Experiences create growth, wisdom, and compassion.

Deep Emotions and Privacy

All human beings have three lives: public, private, and secret.
– Gabriel García Márquez

Eighth house people are not surface-level people. They crave connections and seek depth in relationships. Superficiality annoys them and pushes them away. They avoid small talk and prefer deep, meaningful conversations that touch their soul. Feeling a connection with other people is a priority. Loners at heart, they would prefer to do things alone than with others who are not on their level. Having privacy is important and they dislike feeling exposed or forced to talk. They prefer to live in the shadows lurking behind the scenes. The main reason they feel this way is due to their highly empathic and sensitive nature. Being around people in social situations can be emotionally stressful. This is one reason they like to have privacy and need to spend time alone.

Eighth house people are born with strong perceptive abilities and enjoy watching others from a distance. They have an ability to size people up and see through the surface-level persona that others share. Even though they crave an emotional connection, it can be draining for them. This is because they feel everything going on in the environment and absorb other people's energy. Natural born psychologists, they are born with a gift of listening to other people's problems and giving wise advice. They need time to withdraw socially to recover from stress. It is important that they make time for self-care activities and replenish their own energy. Projecting energy around them happens naturally because of the powerful intensity of this house. This can be a double-edged sword because they can find that their vitality is lessened. They can get tired easily due to this ability to give energy without even realizing it.

Eighth house people must balance their intense emotions. Emotions come on strong like crashing waves. Making time to regenerate their energy is critical. Brooding is common if they don't get adequate private time. Experiencing sadness, irritability, and depression can be a struggle.

Most eighth house people that I have met in person and online in my eighth house astrology group can be distrusting of others. They are observers watching from the shadows. It takes them time to open up and share their intense emotional side. The last thing they want to do is feel vulnerable with someone they can't trust. They love strongly but can also go into fight or flight mode, cutting off everything and everyone around them. Hibernating for hours, days, months, even years hidden away in a room where they can dwell on what they feel is a common behavior. They become obsessed with their inner world of emotions and constantly like to relive painful experiences. Feeling pain makes them feel alive so they tend to hold onto their painful emotions and purposely force themselves to continually feel them. This can turn into obsession and rumination on negative things. Some eighth house clients have shared with me the urge to self-harm through cutting. They explain to me that it's difficult to feel their emotions or that they want to feel something because they feel numb. This is a dangerous behavior that needs to be healed. Talking to a counselor can help you get connected to the deeper issue of why this urge manifests itself.

An eighth house client shared with me that he has periods of deep depression and times where he can't even form words to express how he is feeling. He pushes everyone away and spends time alone in a dark room where he reads, sleeps, and journals. His wife dislikes this personality trait and worries about him. When he goes through these periods they often argue and it puts stress on his marriage. He explained to me if he did not have time to dwell and be alone, he would not come out of his dark moods. He is a Capricorn Sun in the eighth house along with Neptune. Once he recharges, his mood changes and he is able to come back out into the world again. He is ready to communicate and act like the person his family knows him to be.

It is important for eighth house people to accept themselves and be able to express their needs. They need to find healthy outlets that work for them even if they seem dark and scary to those closest to them. They know themselves best and what helps to handle their intense emotional nature. Being patient with themselves is important. Struggling to explain themselves to others can cause greater stress and anxiety. Sometimes they can't find the words to adequately explain how they feel. If you have someone close to you with eighth house planets try to remember they are trying to survive in a world where they feel everything intensely and profoundly, and it can be painful. Be patient with them and allow them time to cope and be supportive when they are going through a darker period. Understand that they need privacy because this encourages them to process things faster. Healing behind the scenes works for them. Other people are not always able to help eighth house people and there is a reason for this. They are designed to dig deep within themselves and find their own answers. This is part of their karmic learning and spiritual journey.

Mastering the public, private, and secret side of life is the goal. They are able to juggle different personas and portray themselves in public differently than they really are in private. Eighth house people tend to be introverts but others might perceive them as extroverted. Many people believe they truly know eighth house people but would be surprised to realize the lives they live behind the scenes. Secret hobbies and interests are sacred to them. They cherish them enough to keep them private and close to their hearts. Only those who are trusted will ever see the personal and secret side of their lives. Those that are chosen and allowed into their inner sanctum are lucky and should appreciate the honor.

Chapter Four

Intense Relationships & Sexuality and Intimacy

The meeting of two personalities is like the contact of two chemical substances: if there is any reaction, both are transformed.
– Carl Jung

Intense Relationships

When I love someone, I become obsessed and have a hard time letting go.
– S.B.

Eighth house people are known to be intense in relationships. When planets are placed in the eighth, there is a need to experience passion and intimacy with another person. They find themselves entangled in intense relationships, sometimes toxic and unhealthy ones, where they feel overwhelming emotions. When they love, they love hard. It is difficult for them to connect physically with someone unless they feel strong feelings, physical attraction and passion. Getting involved in unhealthy and destructive relationships is common because it helps them feel alive. Intimate relationships teach them a lot about commitment, trust, and loyalty.

When eighth house people feel strong emotions for another person, they can have a hard time letting them go. It takes them longer than most to allow people into their lives, and once they do beware, because they don't take it lightly. Eighth house people are known to be possessive, jealous, and controlling. When things are going well, they are one hundred percent committed. If things go wrong, they are known to cut people off completely. They have a hard time being friends with someone they had feelings for or a sexual relationship with. Relationships are all or nothing for them. The influence of Pluto intensifies these instincts to possess or discard. Lukewarm emotions are not part of their personality. They crave intensity and often get very attached to those they care about. These feelings can quickly swing to anger, revenge, and hate if they feel hurt. Being betrayed is one of their greatest fears.

It is important that eighth house people create a balance in relationships. Understanding themselves and facing difficult emotional patterns is part of their learning. Facing fears of being vulnerable will help them develop stronger relationships in the long run. They transform and heal themselves through love, trust, and commitment. Relationships bring out positive and negative personality traits that they often hide deep within. Accepting how they feel and making time to work on problems early will help. Cutting people off and walking away too early can cause regrets. All or nothing thinking can cause a lot of pain and regrets. It is important for eighth house people to learn to balance overwhelming feelings which creates greater harmony in their lives. They learn a lot about themselves through intimate relationships and learning to trust others.

Sexuality and Intimacy

I am sexually dead I do believe. I think my choices in men have all been terrible, and I have never really had a strong mind-body-sexual experience. I have ached for it in my soul, but somehow it eludes me. The wrong types of men always find me. I must radiate energy that says, "I am perfect if you want to take advantage of a woman."
– Female, U.S.A.

The eighth house is associated with sexuality and deep intimacy. It is not about casual sex but deep soul connections and sexual bonding. The fifth house is associated with lighthearted sexual activity and short-term love affairs. When eighth house people have sexual intercourse with someone, they feel forever bonded to them. It is extremely painful for them to let go of or end relationships if they share intimacy. After talking with eighth house people, I have found that this sexual energy can manifest in two different ways. First, there can be a highly sexual nature and high sex drive, which can push them to have sex at a young age. Eighth house people are not afraid to talk about sex and they have a fascination with the process of birth. Some are very open and confident when it comes to seeking intimacy. There can be an arrogance at times depending on which sign is on the eighth house cusp because they know they are attractive and that others are magnetically drawn to them. They can also be reckless and experience an unhealthy balance. Some use sex as a weapon or as part of a game to play with others. Some might pursue those who are a challenge or who play hard to get. This behavior can backfire on them creating painful karma. Being responsible with their powerful sexual energy is important to avoid hurting themselves and others. Developing healthy relationships is an important lesson to learn. The second type of eighth house person is someone who often restricts the sexual urge and they can live a life of celibacy for many years. There is an all-or-nothing feeling regarding sexual desires and experiences. I find that eighth house people are either very sexual when they are in relationships or there is no sex at all, even celibacy. Some feel this need is never fulfilled and it is difficult for them to find attraction to others that ignites deep passion. Many eighth house people share with me they have chosen a life of celibacy. Repression of the sexual urges and needs can last for months and years. Due to not meeting the right people in relationships they choose being alone. These two polarities are common themes eighth house people and clients have shared with me.

Eighth house people need to feel soul connections in order to have sex with someone. Many clients have shared with me that if they don't feel a strong emotional bond, then they are not physically attracted to someone. They won't even want to be touched or kissed by someone if they don't feel that connection. One situation that transpires is that they can get involved in unhealthy relationships with toxic partners. Falling in love with people that have unhealed pain, trauma, addiction, and abuse issues from their childhood is common. Relationship partners do not always treat them with respect. Trusting others enough to have a physical connection can be challenging if there are unhealed childhood issues. When they feel betrayed, they can experience additional trauma which creates a wounding cycle. This pattern can replay throughout their life and it's a karmic lesson from the past that needs to be healed.

My research revealed that many eighth house people experience a sexual wound. Some experienced a type of sexual abuse when they were a child. They often felt their trust was broken or they were taken advantage of by someone they cared about. This can happen in childhood, or early adulthood, and it often manifests in intimate relationships. Feeling victimized in relationships is a common eighth house theme. This can happen when someone they love is unfaithful, lies to them, or uses them for sex. They may perceive that they were used for sex and if they trusted and loved someone these feelings are extremely hard to let go of. Sexual abuse and trauma can occur when the planets Pluto, Mars, or Uranus are placed in the eighth house. Aspects to other planets can also influence this energy for positive or negative outcomes. There are sometimes family secrets surrounding incest or abuse of some kind that could involve other family members, siblings, cousins, or grandparents. Wounding might also come from a friend, neighbor, family friend, or through community connections with people from school or church. I had a client who was sexually abused by his priest when he was a boy and never told a soul until he was in his 60s. Wounds can manifest physically, emotionally, or psychologically and affect the ability to have true physical intimacy. Communication problems in personal relationships is also common. Difficulties trusting others can happen due to insecurities, and a pattern of shutting people out due to fears of being hurt.

A lack of trust and cautiousness prevents eighth house people from opening up their body, mind, and soul fully to other people. They often feel lonely, unless they have a partner that is on their same level energy-wise and similar soul-wise. Friendships are rare because they are selective about who they allow into their lives. The quality is more important to eighth house people than the quantity. One or two close friends is common and they are grateful for the people who they know they can trust.

Some eighth house people can develop reckless sexual behavior trying to seek a soul connection. Many have shared with me that they had contracted sexually transmitted diseases and had unprotected sex in their younger days. These unstable relationships can increase emotional trauma and bring out unhealthy relationship patterns. Eighth house people are passionate partners and possess a sexual energy that attracts others. Their intensity can be felt strongly even when they are silent. Others see them as magnetic and attractive, and are extremely drawn to them physically. It is important that they recognize the power they have over others and realize they attract certain types of personalities based on their own unhealed pain. Looking at the sign on the eighth house cusp can reveal the types of people they are sexually attracted to. For instance, for me I have Aries on the eighth house cusp as well as several planets there. The people from my past who hurt me are the same ones I had the greatest attraction to. They both were Aries Sun individuals.

Sexuality and intimacy go hand in hand. Trust is critical for a deeper relationship to develop. There is a difference between sex and true intimacy. Recognizing relationship patterns and realizing how important they are in overcoming challenges with eighth house energy will help bring greater balance into your life. Self-awareness is key in maneuvering healthy relationships. Transforming through sexual intimacy and embracing healthy relationships will create transformation, resilience and strengthen the way eighth house people love.

Chapter Five

Karma and Past Lives

I remember having images flashing in my mind when I was a child.
I was swimming in the ocean and I drowned. I was always afraid
of water and I think that in a past life I must have drowned. I even
dreamed of this person drowning and it felt so real, I know it's me.
– Male, U.S.A.

The eighth house is associated with past lives and karma. Karma is the belief that the energy and experiences that we have created with other people in prior lifetimes affects our current life experiences. Our thoughts, words, and actions affect our karmic lessons with others. These energies have to be balanced. Karmic experiences can manifest in both positive and negative ways. When planets are in the eighth house dealing with other people is often the greatest challenge. Those we have harmed and those who have harmed us tend to come back into our inner circle. Karma with family, friends, coworkers, and acquaintances is associated with the eighth house. Experiencing betrayal, emotional pain, and learning forgiveness is crucial for balancing out this energy.

Experiences with others feels fated and destined. There seems to be a common thread in the lives of eighth house people where they experience unexplained attractions with certain people. They feel they must pursue these feelings and learn more about them. These intense experiences help them grow and balance out past karma. When they feel strong attractions there is no one who can stop them in finding out what the connection is. They need to be careful about destroying their life in the process. Sometimes karma is playing out and painful things from the past just need to be allowed to be felt, and then let go of, or avoided.

Confusion happens when eighth house people think they need to change their lives based on these strong attractions. They may believe it's destiny. Feeling deep emotions can motivate them to pursue paths that are detrimental. They can find themselves trapped in a cycle of traumatic and abusive relationships. It is important that eighth house people step back from emotions and think more practically before making major life changes. Learning patience and not acting on passion alone is important.

An eighth house client shared with me an intense past life experience that replayed in this lifetime. When she was getting energy work done, she was in a deep relaxed state and had the most vivid memory come to her. She saw herself as a male in the old west and she saw another male who she knew was her grandfather in this life. She had always wondered why her grandfather had sacrificed his finances to ensure she could go to college. There was guilt and a sense of burden that she felt at times. She felt she owed her grandparents and wanted to pay them back because of how much they helped her. This was a karmic pattern she had to deal with, accept, and heal. In this memory that flashed in front of her eyes she saw a man pull a rifle and they were going to shoot the man who was her grandfather. She lodged herself in front of him and was shot. She saved his life. She saw herself as a man lying on the floor of a tavern bleeding. She started crying and came out of the experience. The energy healer asked her what she saw and she explained to him the intense memory. This was the first past life memory she had ever experienced. Many years later she shared with me that something very traumatic happened to her and it involved her grandfather.

Her grandfather had been struggling after the loss of his wife and a recent breakup with a woman he had been dating. His health was suffering and her mother was concerned there was more going on with him. The client told me she was asked to go to their hometown to his home because he was going to move into an independent living facility. She arrived at her grandfather's house and the family was there to see what furniture he wanted them to have. She felt sick to her stomach and was sad that this was happening. She sat in the living room waiting for him to arrive with her father. When he walked in, he seemed different and his eyes had a strange look to them. He came in and started telling everyone what he wanted them to have and had a very specific list. She watched him walk into his bedroom and she followed him. He went to the side of the bed and she saw him pull a handgun out of the drawer and put it in his pocket. She was shocked and he quickly walked out. She went and told her mother that her grandfather was acting strange and he put this gun in his sweatpants pocket. Her mother and uncle both looked at each other and they told her he was fine. She told them that someone needed to get the gun away from him.

Suddenly, he tells them all in the living room that he was ready to leave and wanted to be taken back to his nursing facility. She stood up and followed him out the door to the garage and her mother followed. Her father pulls up in his truck, and her uncle comes out into the garage with them. Her grandfather got in the passenger seat of the truck and her dad was driving. She tells her mother and uncle, someone needs to get the gun from him. She knew he was depressed and was not acting like himself. Her mother started crying. She did not want her brother to be the one to get the gun because they were finally getting along. They had not had a good relationship. She stood there and neither of them were going to do anything or follow him.

She followed him to the truck where he was sitting next to her father. Her father had no idea what was going on or that her grandfather a gun in his pocket. She asked her grandfather to give her the gun and explained that he can't take that back to the nursing facility. He refused and would not look at her. She continued to get upset and started crying begging for him to give her the gun. He had his hand on it and would not let go of it. She continued to try to get him to release the gun from his pocket, struggling with him and he finally released his grip. She took the gun from him and walked inside. She told her mother and uncle to get all the guns out of the house. It was evident that he was not doing well and was having suicidal thoughts. The mother was devastated but agreed. Her uncle was making light of it and believed he was just wanting attention.

She left to return home to prepare for a work trip. She traveled to a conference on Sunday the day after this happened. On Monday during the conference her mother kept calling her cell phone. She was worried something was wrong so she walked out into the hallway to call her mother. The phone rang and her mother answered and cried, "Your grandfather shot himself and he is being air evacuated to the hospital for surgery." She froze in disbelief, asking herself how this could have happened. Didn't they get all the guns out of the house after what happened on Saturday! She shared with me that her grandfather had hidden a small handgun in the mattress of his bed. She then asked how he ended up alone in the house and was even able to do this. Apparently, her uncle had taken him to the doctor and he asked for him to take him to his house to get something out of the basement. The uncle innocently did this not knowing there was any further danger in the house but when he went downstairs, he heard two gun shots go off. He ran upstairs and saw his father lying there. He had shot himself in the chest twice but both bullets went through his lungs and out. The amazing part of the story was that he survived, had lung surgery due to sepsis, and is doing well today. It was a miracle. This eighth house client felt that it was strange to see this gun situation play out again in this life. She immediately remembered the vivid past life memory she had years before involving a gun. Another interesting part of the story is that her grandfather had the South Node in the eighth house and Saturn.

This client's Moon is in the eighth house in the sign Aries and it is interesting that this was her mother's father and the Moon represents the mother or maternal side of the family chart. Aries rules violence, guns, weapons, and impulsivity.

One thing I have noticed in my own life and with clients is that there is something special about eighth house people. When someone hurts, betrays, or abandons them they might feel like they will never hear from them again. I have learned that karma is very strong with eighth house people and every person that hurts them eventually comes back. It might be months, years, or decades but the very person who abused them returns to apologize. This pattern is very evident in my research with eighth house clients. I have been shocked to see this happen in my own life. Every single person who betrayed or treated me badly in the past always returned. They would contact me years later crying, sad, depressed, and say how sorry they were that they hurt me. At first it was a shock but I saw this pattern play out throughout my life. Many eighth house people share similar experiences with karmic relationships. It can actually be cathartic and extremely healing when this happens. It is like the universe sends those that caused you pain back into your life to help you forgive and heal.

Traumatic life situations manifest unexpectedly and these experiences can be hard to adjust to. These experiences happen to encourage eighth house people to heal and develop strength. Forgiving others and letting go of stagnant energy from the past is an important part of healing karmic lessons. It is beneficial for eighth house people to recognize that when they have difficulties with certain people they need to remember there is often a past life lesson to learn. Recognizing recurring patterns that are replaying in their lives will help them learn spiritual lessons once and for all.

Chapter Six

Death, Loss, Endings, Rebirth, and Regeneration

Suffering is an ineradicable part of life, even as fate and death. Without suffering and death, human life cannot be complete.
– Viktor E. Frankl

One of the greatest tests an eighth house person experiences is the death of someone close to them. Those with eighth house planets have a connection with death that starts in early childhood. Certain eighth house placements can reveal how loss will impact your life. The subject of death can be uncomfortable for most people. Death is a taboo subject. Things that are uncomfortable for most people to talk about, such as grief and loss, are associated with the eighth house. When we lose a loved one, it forces us to question our purpose on this earth. It brings up many unanswered questions and fears about life after death and the existence of the soul. To stare death in the eye and confront it comes naturally for eighth house people. They had no other choice but to face death because it was forced on them.

Many clients have shared with me that ever since they were a child they would lay in bed at night and think to themselves, "What if I die?" They wonder where they would go, if it would hurt to die, if their physical body would rot away in a casket, and if their soul would live on. Thoughts of loss and endings haunted their minds. Eighth house people know they will not live forever. This fact pushes them to study religion, astrology, metaphysics, and mystical subjects. They want to figure out the meaning of life and make sense of the tragedies that surround them.

Death is a difficult topic and a painful area of life that most normal people do not want to talk about. When eighth house people realize that death involves mourning, they can see the devastating impact loss has on those around them. They become very aware and sensitive to other people's grief. They serve as the strong family member that supports everyone else who is grieving. As natural healers they help family and loved ones who face saying goodbye and letting go. They are the ones who are strong enough to give the eulogy about the lost loved one while holding back their own tears. Endings rule the eighth house and this is an area of life that they become comfortable with at an early age. Life is change and they know it on an instinctual level. Eighth house people grow stronger and more resilient through these experiences.

Uncomfortable Topic

Many of us are taught from an early age to fear death. Deadening silences, uncomfortable body language, and facial expressions often occur when we bring this topic up for discussion. A personal example that I like to share is when I attended a family funeral several years ago. Someone in our family died unexpectedly and many people were shocked by this loss. I took my daughter to the funeral with me and it was her first funeral. Let me mention that she has Pluto in her eighth house and is a Scorpio South Node so she has eighth house energy. She kept pointing at the casket and asked me to take her up there. I hesitated at first because I did not want to expose her to this taboo, secret universal truth at such a young age. Instead, I tried to convince her to go see her cousin. My daughter being an eighth house person adamantly refused and wanted to go to the casket. At four years old she was very curious and wanted answers. She kept asking me why people were crying.

I walked up to the casket with her. She saw a man lying in the casket and she watched him. She asked, "What is wrong with him, Momma?" Someone was standing next to us and immediately said, "He is sleeping, honey." The uncomfortable silence and the look on my daughter's face is something I will never forget. I felt bad for this man who just lost his only brother. I know that sometimes little white lies are all we can come up with in the midst of grief. It helps us survive, cope, and carry on. It brings us peace and comfort to explain death in a positive way. Eighth house people have an interest in ghosts, spirits, and the afterlife. Some share with me that they even have experienced near death experiences. They believe in the existence of a soul because they have witnessed firsthand what happens when they leave their physical body. Many have astral projected or had traumatic experiences that verified the existence of a soul. This life is not the end. There is a purpose to why we are here.

Connected to Death

Being connected to death can manifest in many different ways. It might come through a dream, gut instinct, or a strong intuition that something is going to happen to someone close to them. Some people share with me dreams that prepare them for the loss of someone close to them. Shedding light on eighth house issues is one way to master its lessons. Eighth house people have a common bond and are connected to the mystical universe that exists beyond the physical realm. Many clients have shared with me fears of dying young or experiencing a tragic death of a parent because of the eighth house. I receive e-mails from people all over the world who are worried about having planets in this house. Negative interpretations about the eighth house still exist but through my research I have realized that loss can also create positive growth, emotional healing, and psychological strength. Death of the personality, identity, emotions, and beliefs is also a common experience. Through these intense experiences, an eighth house person is reborn, transformed, and grows into an entirely new person who accepts their spiritual gifts.

Traditionally the sign on the cusp of the eighth house and

planets there can show where and how losses might occur. It can also point to the manner of death and how one might die. For instance, if Aries is on the eighth house cusp, death could be due to impulsive behavior, fire, disagreements, car accidents, and head injuries. Capricorn there shows a long life and death from natural causes. This is the energy, but we always have free will and choice. My belief is that some things are destined to happen and meant to be regardless of what we do. I like to focus on the positive energy of this house and how connecting to death is something that heals eighth house people. It reminds me of a television show I watched recently where a girl witnessed her father being murdered as a teenager. She grew up and became a death doula, helping those who were in hospice cross over to the other side. Providing that nurturing care to someone on the threshold of life and death is such an eighth house thing. I thought to myself that character had to be an eighth house person.

Seeking questions that are hard to answer is an eighth house thing. I remember asking my parents why we had to die. I wanted to know exactly how it would affect me personally. They could not answer these questions for me. This led me to pursue my own set of answers. As a person with the Moon, Jupiter and Chiron in the eighth house I realized death is an inevitable part of life. I dread these sad days so I try to live my life with kindness and compassion. We are souls and not physical bodies. The soul lives on and survives after death. This is something that I believe and it brings comfort. I truly believe this after hearing all the amazing stories that eighth house people have shared with me about death, loss, rebirth, and healing. To die and be reborn is part of being a phoenix.

Some eighth house people have told me that they have not been personally affected by physical death. Very rarely I have met clients who did not lose a loved one at a young age. Although I often see they are impacted by emotional and psychological deaths, and rebirths throughout their lives. Psychological death is as intense and painful as the physical loss of a loved one. It can be difficult to release emotional burdens that need cleansing. It is hard to allow our personality to be stripped away and force ourselves to change. This is why regeneration is associated with the eighth house. Transforming as a person after heartache makes eighth house people wise beyond their years.

Personal Experiences with Death

As an eighth house person, I have experienced many tragic, unexpected deaths of people close to me. My first experience with death happened when I was in high school in 1992. I was starting my senior year and had a close friend who was going to be a sophomore. We were hanging out a lot that summer. That summer she had recently spent the night at my house. The next day something strange happened. At this time, I worked for the Parks and Recreation in my small town and managed the concession stands, batting cages, and kept score at softball games. While working at the concession stand that night, she came up to talk to me. Something seemed different about her. I had a strange feeling come over me. I was only 16 years old and did not understand my intuition or fully trust it at that time. She told me she was not happy with her current friend group and was looking forward to hanging out with me and my friends once school started. She was at the ballpark with some of her friends and I watched her walk off into the distance.

She was playing catch with a boy we went to school with. I remember watching her and something bothered me. I remember it felt like I was observing her in slow motion, almost like a dream in the distance. As I watched her, I had an uncomfortable feeling inside. I closed up for the night and went home. I came into work the next day and it was a ghost town. All the soccer games were cancelled and I didn't know what was happening. The manager was not there and I saw a young boy sitting at a picnic table. He seemed sad. He saw me, walked over and I asked, "Where is everybody?" He said, "Your friend died last night in an accident." I said, "No. There is no way." He went on to tell me it was in the newspaper that morning and she was killed. I froze and felt sick. I called my mother and she said to come home.

It was on the front page of the newspaper that she had been accidentally shot that very night after we talked. Apparently, some young teenage boys in our town had stolen a gun out of one of their dad's trucks. They had been passing the gun around amongst each other. This had been going on for a couple of weeks but none of them told their parents. The parent did not report the gun stolen. Unfortunately, my friend was riding in the passenger seat and the girl driving was dating one of these boys. The two boys were in the backseat of the car and had secretly brought the gun with them. They thought they took all the bullets out of the gun and that it was empty. What they did not realize was that there was a bullet left in the chamber. According to investigators they were playing with the gun in the backseat and it accidentally went off. The bullet went through the passenger seat through my friend's heart and killed her instantly. It was terrible and it took me a long time to accept it. I had never known anyone who had died and it was the first funeral I ever attended.

Tragic Death

This experience encouraged me to seek the meaning of life. I started studying astrology and researching spiritual topics which is why I became a social worker. I wanted to help others who experienced trauma. No one is immune to death. Everyone eventually loses someone close to them. First, we experience shock, and then disbelief. It can take time to accept the reality of our new life without the person we cared about. From 2018 to the present I have experienced several losses. In 2019, a few days before Thanksgiving my husband's father passed away unexpectedly. This loss affected us emotionally and financially. Then in February 2020, I was traveling for work and was contacted by an old college friend who told me she thought our mutual friend Maria was shot and killed at a community center where she worked as a manager in St. Louis. It was all over the news but they had not released who the victim of the shooting was for a few days.

When I returned from my trip, I found out that it was my friend who was tragically killed. There was a janitor that worked at the community center who walked up to the front counter and she happened to be there and he shot her. Someone was able to escape out the front door and an off-duty police officer happened to be outside in the parking lot. There were about 150 people in the community center at the time. The police officer saved many lives but my friend Maria was the only person who was killed. This was such a tragedy and when I watched it on the news it felt like a movie or a dream. A few days before her memorial, her father died within a week of her death. It was a very difficult time because the coronavirus pandemic had started across the world and this was right before the shutdown.

In June 2020 one of my colleagues and friend died unexpectedly. I had just spoken to her on the phone for an hour a few weeks prior to this. I received a call that she had a brain aneurysm and had to have emergency brain surgery. She did not survive the surgery and passed away after being on life support for a few days. It was upsetting because we could not attend the funeral due to the coronavirus pandemic. There was a zoom set up for those who were not immediate family to watch the funeral but it was not the same. I did not feel like I had closure or was able to say goodbye. This past year there was a memorial stone dedicated to her at the installation she worked at and our entire team held a team building activity there. I was able to say a prayer for her and meet her two sons and husband. There were many tears cried but it was also comforting that we were able to say a formal goodbye and honor her memory.

I want to help people heal and learn to grieve in healthy ways. Death is inevitable and these experiences have intensified the awareness that we will all die someday. I try to live in the present moment and I know how precious life is. In the blink of an eye everything can change. It is important to cherish and appreciate our family and friends. Eighth house people are strong and capable of handling their own grief and also able to help others. We understand death because we have looked death in the eye. These cycles teach us that death is just a transition into the next realm. We all have different beliefs about what happens after death. I do not believe that death is the end and this gives me hope. All of those people we have lost are still with us in spirit.

Chapter Seven

Healing & Forgiveness

Forgiveness is giving up the hope that the past could have been any different, it's accepting the past for what it was, and using this moment and this time to help yourself move forward.
– Oprah Winfrey

Eighth house people often feel they have been wounded by life, people and circumstances. They are brutally aware of the pain that comes with loss. The most important thing to learn from these experiences is how to forgive. People need others that can truly understand their pain. The best counselors and healers are those that have suffered themselves.

Eighth house people are wounded healers and attract people that have similar wounds. These wounds might be loss, some type of abuse, grief, guilt, anger, distrust, and depression. The purpose of pain is to enable us to grow and learn important life lessons. There is a reason that people come into our lives. We need to embrace the valuable learning experiences that we encounter. One of the hardest things for eighth house people to do is to truly forgive others. They may believe they have forgiven others, but many times deep within their soul they carry the painful memories of past hurts. They can repress uncomfortable feelings and secretly refuse to deal with them.

Memories will be triggered at times leading to negative emotions. Eighth house people blame themselves for past actions and mistakes. The past is over and our actions cannot be taken back. Choose to forgive, release, and heal. This can be very difficult to hear. I know it is not easy, but it is necessary for eighth house people to survive in this world. If eighth house people want to truly heal then they must forgive.

How do we forgive?

The first step in forgiveness is looking deeper at what makes you feel angry, hurt, and betrayed. Are you upset by a situation? Or a person who mistreated you? Take time to sit down and journal your thoughts and feelings. Write down as much as you can about what feelings come up and things you want to let go of. We all need to accept that we are not perfect and that everyone makes mistakes. Living a perfect life is not possible, so we can only start in the present moment in order for change to happen.

Baby Steps for Letting Go

We can take small baby steps towards changing our behaviors. When we feel stuck in our own negative feelings, it is important to realize that we are human and have every right to feel the way we do. It is easy to blame others for our unhappiness, but we are the only ones who have control over how we react and respond to challenges. We do not forgive others for them; we forgive others for ourselves. When we hold onto anger, resentment, and pain we are only hurting ourselves. It is not an easy thing to forgive. It takes great bravery and strength to be the bigger person.

Eighth house people are stronger than most people. They are survivors. Remember that the only thing you have control over is your own mind. This is a key factor in the healing process. Rewards and blessings happen when you finally release things that are holding you back. Pain will evaporate like mist when they finally release everything. It takes great courage, character, determination, and stamina to successfully master planets placed in this house. Don't think it will be easy or occur overnight. It might take years to truly heal from the past and that is perfectly fine. Eighth house people just need to remember to take steps in the right direction at the speed they are comfortable with. If you have something to forgive, start the process today. Seize the moment and allow the process of forgiveness to bloom. Be patient with yourself and others. All you have to do is make the decision to change.

Releasing the Past

Holding onto feelings from the past keeps us stuck in the healing process. It is important for eighth house people to truly let go of the people, thoughts, emotions, and behaviors that have kept them from healing themselves. They have to truly release things on a deeper level. If they are still thinking about a past lover or abusive relationship, they have to release it.

Many eighth house people tell me that they want to let go of the past but struggle. Experiencing loss at a young age is a shared eighth house experience. This often haunts them throughout their lives. They need to realize that losing a parent or loved one happened for a reason. The most basic way eighth house people can let go of the past is to find productive ways to move forward. An exercise that I share with clients involves fire. I encourage you to write down all of your feelings and thoughts on a piece of paper. Gather up a picture of the person you are upset with. After you write everything down light it on fire and let it burn. Use safety when you burn it and truly allow it to be released. Another thing which can help release the past is to bury something in the ground. You can write down how you feel, include a photo or possession that reminds you of the person or situation and bury it in the ground. Release it and walk away.

Denying Feelings

I recommend getting a massage once a week, energy healing sessions, do some intense cardio workouts, and eat healthy. All of these things can help eighth house people on their journey of letting go. I always find energy healing sessions very helpful because they help me get in touch with emotions that I have buried. Emotional pain and physical pain are connected. Eighth house people tend to shut out their feelings and deny their problems. The issue is that the eighth house will expose hidden things and bring them to light. We cannot avoid unpleasant emotions forever.

The best way to heal is to stop running from problems and face the pain. You have to confront the demons to be able to truly let them go once and for all. It is helpful for eighth house people to seek therapy and counseling from a professional. I highly recommend finding someone to talk to about addictions, grief, and anger. Unhealed emotions can create illnesses in the physical body. Diseases of the sexual organs such as cysts on the uterus, ovaries, urinary tract infections, prostate cancer, and bowel issues are common in people with eighth house planets.

Blessings and Challenges

The first thing I share with eighth house clients is that they have a difficult chart, but there are many blessings that come from overcoming challenges. Bottom line is that eighth house people will have a harder life than most. It is the karma that they have chosen to experience this lifetime. I believe through my research that eighth house people have resisted growth in previous lifetimes. They chose a more difficult path this time around because they knew that if they didn't, they would continue to play it safe and seek security.

There may be periods of rest for eighth house people, but they usually do not last very long. They need to accept that their path is meant to be filled with crisis and change. They are not being punished by the universe even if they feel that way sometimes. They must seek a spiritual connection to help overcome difficulties. The most important thing an eighth house person needs to remember is that they must accept their faults, negative personality traits, depressive emotions, and unhealthy behaviors. They have chosen to be a healer in this lifetime. The best way we can truly heal others is when we have lived through difficult situations and emerged with greater experience. Destined to do this, eighth house people are supposed to use their gifts to help guide others. Eighth house people need to accept that they are wounded healers.

Finding a Spiritual Connection

Eighth house people benefit by finding a spiritual connection in their lives. Overcoming adversities and painful emotional experiences can be difficult. Without a spiritual belief system eighth house people can become despondent, withdrawn, shut off, depressed, and feel cut off. Eighth house people often feel lonely. Being born with feelings of loneliness and a deep need to merge with others is a constant balancing act. Feeling different and even like an outsider in their own family and with friends is common. Eighth house people are special and have a unique mission here on this earth.

I believe that you are either born spiritual or you become spiritual through suffering. Most spiritual teachers have suffered and struggled with adversity. Many people that are religious leaders had a painful childhood and a lot of loss in their lives. If our lives were perfect, we would never grow. Suffering increases eighth house people's spiritual abilities and psychic gifts. Eighth house people will never be fulfilled through career success and financial stability. They always find these lacking and this awareness pushes them to seek deep relationships. They are meant to transform feelings of separateness into feelings of oneness by learning to trust others.

Trusting Others

Trust is something that many people believe they have until someone disappoints them. Trusting others is usually effortless when we are younger because we are naïve and only see the good in people. It is not until someone betrays us that we feel pain and realize the truth. That pain is a constant reminder that we could be hurt again. Human beings do not want to feel pain. They attempt to shut themselves off from others to protect themselves. Eighth house people hold onto deep wounds regarding trust and intimacy. I know many eighth house people who have told me that it is easier being alone. This is a way they protect themselves from heartache. Every eighth house person I know has withdrawn and cut people out of their lives at some point. They would rather hide behind the scenes and be by themselves because it is easier.

It is important to remember that through connections with people we heal and are able to heal others. Eighth house people are required to use their gifts this lifetime. Avoiding reality is only going to make things worse. It is healthy to withdraw from others sometimes to recover, recuperate, and gain more energy to face the world. It is also important for eighth house people to remember that they don't have to tell everyone all their secrets. They don't have to be friends with everyone, they can be selective. Eighth house people need to realize that people will hurt them and it's unavoidable. Giving people a chance and risking the possibility of getting hurt helps them step out of their comfort zone. Sometimes you just have to step out there, dust yourself off and try again.

Being Vulnerable

Learning to be vulnerable goes hand in hand with trust. Eighth house people do not like to feel vulnerable or admit their weaknesses to others. It is important for eighth house people to let down the strong wall they have built up around themselves. They don't have to do this with everyone they meet, but it is important for them to find one or two people in their life that they can be honest with. Vulnerability is not meant to be perceived as a weakness. It is a strength as long as it is used with the right people. Eighth house people have to have some trust with someone in order to feel comfortable with being open. Taking baby steps in the direction of trust will enable eighth house people to truly share who they are with another human being.

Taking Care of Yourself

The bottom line is that many eighth house people are used to taking care of everyone else and they often sacrifice themselves for others. Eighth house people have to practice self-reflection and have a constant awareness of how they are feeling. They need to pamper themselves and pursue self-care activities that are useful. Focusing on being present in their physical body, centering, and practicing mindfulness can help them feel better. Writing down a list of goals and things they want to achieve can be helpful. This gives them something to look forward to. Making sure they pursue activities that bring them joy is important. Spending time doing things that bring peace is important for eighth house people. Carving out time to meditate and practice relaxation exercises encourages the process of healing.

Many eighth house people will benefit from seeking counseling or psychotherapy. It is important for eighth house people to have someone to talk to about their problems. They are insightful, but sometimes believe they have everything figured out. I like to encourage them to open up their minds and realize that others have insights that may be helpful for them. They don't have to suffer in silence or be their own therapist. Another thing eighth house people need to remember is that it takes time to heal. Time heals all wounds even if it does not feel that way at first. It is important for them to treat themselves with kindness and patience. Allow enough time to heal the wounds of the past. Letting go can take time, and eighth house people can take as much time as they need.

Embracing Your Shadow

It is true that eighth house people see the darkness in the world. At some time in an eighth house person's life, they realize that they have a darkness within. The darkness might express itself as negative thoughts, taboo feelings, unexplained emotions, and controlling behaviors. These feelings are natural for eighth house people and are part of what psychologist Carl Jung called, "the shadow". Jung talked about the shadow as a part of human nature that we hide, repress and try to ignore. I have seen eighth house people attract people that have problems because they are repressing their own dark feelings. They act like a magnet manifesting people that are attracted to the similarities of energy. The shadow part of the personality can't be hidden for long, even though they are naturals at hiding things. An explosion of all the things an eighth house person has done will come bursting out into the open.

It reminds me of Pandora's box, and it has been opened and the eighth house person has to face everything all at once. Once they begin to accept themselves and understand that they have both light and dark within, they can begin to understand the spiritual meaning of life. Every single human being has both light and dark traits. No one is perfect and completely pure all the time. Eighth house people need to embrace their darker side and deal with it. They must embrace all the thoughts, feelings, and behavior patterns they have repressed. Often, they have these behaviors and patterns manifest in their daily lives through other people. These problems can sneak into their relationships and intimacy can be disrupted. My best advice for eighth house people is to embrace their shadow self. Look in the mirror and be completely honest with yourself.

It is hard for anyone to admit they have negative personality traits. Admitting that you have dark parts in yourself creates greater self-awareness. Sometimes the darkness comes from others, but many times the darkness comes from the repressed things we don't want to see in ourselves. I promise that if you embrace the shadow before it unveils itself unexpectedly then your life will be a lot easier. Pain can be avoided by embracing the eighth house shadow and accepting it as part of your life. I recommend studying Carl Jung's theory of the shadow self; it is very enlightening and resonates with many eighth house people.

Chapter Eight

Healer Versus Healed

The person I loved the most betrayed me to the core so now I help others who have been betrayed.
– K.W.

We all have experienced pain or betrayal at some time in our lives. The bitter sting of loss and heartbreak hits us at the core. There are moments you feel like you will never be able to get out of bed. Eighth house people are survivors, and this is the thing I love about them the most. We are strong and I give credit to the energy of Scorpio and Pluto for the ability to recover. We eventually feel anger, and that anger pushes us to fight, to stand up, and get out of bed. We find the strength to rise and face the cold world again.

As eighth house people we can't bear to lose or to let those that hurt us or betray us win or keep us down. We rise. We rise up and survive because it is what we were born to do. It is what we do best. We rise like the phoenix bird out of the ashes of heartache, betrayal, abuse and dismay. We rise up stronger and eager to face the world again. We were born to feel. We were born to heal. We were meant to feel wounded, hurt, betrayed, victimized, belittled, abused, cursed and judged. We had to experience all the darker sides of human nature in the eyes or arms of someone we trusted. Without that type of experience, we would not fulfill our soul mission and destiny.

It is through experiencing pain that eighth house people grow. It is through experiencing deep hurt that we can truly understand the pain of others. The eighth house person is meant to delve into and experience all the deeper emotions under the surface. By experiencing these deeper emotions, we become aware of others' pain, not just our own. When we swim back to the surface we are renewed, transformed and regenerated. We are ready to heal the world.

We attract the wounded like a magnet. Even those who do not realize they are wounded or in need of healing will find their way into an eighth house person's life. They instinctively know that we can help them with their pain. When I was young, people would tell me all their secrets and problems. Even total strangers in the grocery store would approach me and tell me deep, dark, mysterious things. My daughter hates going shopping with me because every time someone starts talking to me and I become a counselor, giving advice, and listening attentively. She does not understand why I continue to listen and give my full attention. She thinks I talk too much and I told her I am being supportive, because I can feel they are lonely.

Once in a candy aisle, an older woman approached me and just blurted out, "My dad just died." Shockingly caught off guard about what she said, she apologized. I calmly told her that I was sorry for her loss. After this experience and many others like it, I realized there was something different about me and my energy. I began to research the eighth house, and interviewed many people with planets here and they had similar experiences. I found kindred spirits and others who had also experienced feeling other people's pain. I learned more about myself from them and the hidden destiny of an eighth house person, which is to follow the path of the healer.

I find that eighth house people are naturally good at healing others, but often neglect their own healing. This hiding will work awhile for an eighth house person and maybe for many years, until something will trigger or unleash what is hidden within to come to the surface to be faced.

There is no greater feeling than the feeling you get when you feel you have helped someone heal. That awareness and deep exchange is beyond words. I lived for that. I lived to serve and experience the satisfaction of healing others. What I did not realize was the immense release and unconditional peace that could come when we allow others to help ourselves heal.

We are blessed when we encounter a special person who touches our eighth house planets and awakens our own pain, but at the same time lifts it without them even knowing it. This creates a process of deep healing within us. I was lucky enough to meet someone who has helped me heal my eighth house energy, merely by listening and being there for me. Exchanging energy and music this person has their Venus and Jupiter conjunct my planets in eighth house. This energy has transformed my pain and helped me grieve and release the past faster than I could have on my own. I will always be grateful to this special friend and they will hold a special place in my heart. I realized that eighth house people must allow themselves to open up to others and experience intimacy. By truly being vulnerable with another person and truly allowing someone into our inner circle we can heal. We can't do it alone. We need others to be a catalyst to push through fears, challenges, and obstacles. Acting as the catalyst for other people's healing, we take the risk of being hurt. Being vulnerable and taking risks means you are strong; they are not signs of weakness. I am thankful for people in my life who have touched my eighth house planets and helped me. Eighth house people do not always experience that kind of reciprocation. We are healers, but there is no greater feeling than that of being healed.

Chapter Nine

Spiritual Gifts and Psychic Abilities

I have three planets in the eighth house. Since I was a boy, I have had strange dreams and a vivid imagination. When I was in bed, I would imagine that I was dead and see myself in a coffin and all my relatives and friends were watching me crying. Some of my dreams come true and are warning of some future situations, but I am not in a position to control them. My sexual instinct is very strong and I love and hate with passion.
– Male, Greece

Many eighth house people share with me that they are sensitive to energy. When planets are placed in the eighth house, there are psychic abilities, spiritual gifts, and an interest in alternative healing modalities such as Reiki, Pranic healing, crystal healing, yoga, and herbal medicine. Helping others heal by studying the energy centers of the body, the chakras, can help eighth house people increase their skills in helping others and themselves. Studying nontraditional medicine and career fields like acupuncture, Ayurveda, and massage therapy will be beneficial.

Some eighth house people have shared with me that they can see auras and colors surrounding others. I had a similar experience myself when I was in college. One day I was at church and when the preacher was doing his sermon, I saw a glowing white light around his head. It surrounded his entire physical body. It looked like another light body surrounding him. Sometimes you might see different colors in the energy field of others. I remember finding it interesting that many churches in Europe and religious art have a halo surrounding Jesus, Mary, Angels, and Buddha. That halo is what is known as the energy field or subtle energetic body that surrounds an individual. This artwork shows the divine energy that radiates from those who are enlightened spiritual figures. It makes me wonder if the historical artists of the past had eighth house planets.

Psychometry

One of the greatest abilities eighth house people are born with is the ability to sense energy. This ability can manifest in many ways. The ability to hold or touch an object and be able to discover information about an event or person is called psychometry. Eighth house people can see memories, experience flashes of images, and experience strong feelings when they touch another person. This can also be experienced when they touch an object of someone who has passed away. They are able to pick up energy from material objects. Some eighth house people are able to connect to missing people by holding objects that belonged to them. Some are able to help law enforcement solve crimes and find missing people. They are sometimes able to confirm if a missing person is dead or alive by holding something personal that belonged to that person. The eighth house is associated with detective work, criminal justice, research, and areas of life that allow them to work behind the scenes. It makes sense that many eighth house people have the ability to tap into these energies and are drawn to these career fields.

A previous client of mine who took Reiki energy healing classes and had several planets in the eighth house shared her experience. When she would lay her hands on a client during a session to send them healing energy, she would pick up their past memories and traumatic memories. If it felt right, she would tell her clients what she saw and they would confirm that it was a real memory from their past. This ability helped many clients heal deep seated pain and unhealed trauma.

Some eighth house people use a pendulum to sense energy. Pendulums can be used to test the energy of objects and even during energy healing sessions. I never knew how, but when I was younger, I had a necklace that had a stone on it. I remember playing with my friend and holding the necklace in the air and asking questions to see if it would move. I did not realize until I was older what a pendulum was used for or even looked like. It is interesting that, somehow, I was aware of energy and using an object to test it. Many eighth house people share similar experiences and an inborn understanding of many metaphysical ideas and processes.

Knowing the Future

Clairvoyance is another popular spiritual gift that eighth house people possess. Eighth house people are born with an ability to understand things that are happening around them. Clairvoyance is the ability to know the future through visions, dreams, and intuition. They often dream deeply and get glimpses of events before they happen in the physical realm. They experience a gut instinct about things that is often right, which validates their intuition. Eighth house people need to listen and trust that voice within. They also need to pay extra attention to their dreams and visions. Learning not to ignore their thoughts, feelings, and hunches about people or situations enhances their trust in their abilities.

Eighth house people share common psychic abilities. Depending on which planets are placed in the eighth house, they will manifest in unique ways. Eighth house people have told me they had dreamed of 9/11, the Japanese tsunami, tornadoes, earthquakes, natural disasters, and fires. They believe that knowing these things were going to happen in advance was a blessing and a curse. The positive part of having these gifts is they can help others. Loneliness and feeling the pain of others can feel like a curse, but it's really a blessing in disguise. Using these special abilities to help others will bring eighth house people a sense of purpose. They are here for a special mission that involves healing. Most eighth house people are interested in doing spiritual work such as astrological counseling, intuitive readings, energy healing, and counseling. The experiences they have will inspire them to study the mysteries of the universe.

Eighth house people are born with telepathy and can pick up other people's thoughts. It can be hard for them to distinguish between their own thoughts and those of others. Their spider senses peak up when someone is being dishonest, angry, or hiding something. Eighth house people are born with a connection to the things that most people feel uncomfortable with.

Experiences with Ghosts, Deceased Loved Ones

Eighth house people have a special energy and aura. They portray an intimidating, strong, and intense presence. This is why people often are drawn to them and share their problems. There is something special about their energy and people do not always understand why they are so attracted to them. Many eighth house people are connected to death and can see spirits, ghosts, and dream of those who have passed on. People who have lost those closest to them are attracted to eighth house people. Loss, grief, and overcoming heartbreak are things eighth house people know well and it's like others sense that they will be able to help them. Experiences with astral projection and near death experiences are common and they might spend time researching the occult. Eighth house people realize they are not just a physical body, but they are spiritual beings.

Many eighth house clients have shared with me that they have sensed the presence of a deceased loved one. Sometimes they report that they wake up and see a parent, grandparent, child, or sibling standing at the foot of their bed. There are times they sense a loved one standing next to them or like someone touching their shoulder. They are connected to death and fascinated by what happens after they die. Eighth house people have shared with me that they either are very afraid of dying or they are not afraid of death at all.

Lucid Dreaming

Eighth house people often share experiences with sleep paralysis and lucid dreaming. Lucid dreaming is waking up inside a dream and realizing you are dreaming. When they first try to fall asleep at night, they often find themselves waking up in their bed and realizing they are mentally awake. When they look at the side of their bed, they often see a person standing there. Sometimes the figure is glowing like a light or shadowy. It can be a stranger or someone close to them. When they realize they are seeing someone they scream and wake up fully. This experience is what some Native American tribes call dream walking. Dream walking is when you are awake inside your own dream. Some people believe there are those who can travel into other people's dreams. Based on my research, I believe that this experience occurs because eighth house people are attached and connected to the astral realm. The astral realm is the closest spiritual realm to earth as discussed in some mystical traditions such as the Kabbalah or the Tree of Life. The Yesod realm is the astral realm that is closest to Malkuth which is the earth realm. Christians also refer to a similar realm and call it purgatory. Many people believe that when we sleep and dream, we are in our astral bodies. The astral body is one of the energy bodies that surround the physical body. It is interesting that when we sleep our brain and body are in a completely relaxed state, where breathing slows down and we fall into deep brain waves. It's almost like we are dead or on the verge of death. Eighth house people dream vividly which explains these astral dream experiences.

One of the hardest things for eighth house people to understand is why these experiences happen to them. Eighth house people find it hard to fall asleep and might leave their bodies without trying to. Many people with the planets Sun, Moon, Neptune, and Pluto in the eighth have shared many intense experiences with me. The reason that eighth house people find these experiences difficult and sometimes traumatic is because they don't have control over them. Pluto rules the eighth house which enhances eighth house people's need to have control over everything and not to feel vulnerable. It makes sense that these experiences are difficult to accept.

Another common experience is mediumship which is the ability to sense or see spirits in the mind or physical realm. This ability reminds me of the abilities of Allison in the television show *Medium*. She would dream about deceased people and the spirit of those who died would be standing at the foot of her bed when she woke up in the night. She would also have flashes or images come into her mind of those who were dead and who were reaching out to her for help. Many eighth house people have experiences like this and struggle to understand how to control them. Eighth house people need to embrace these experiences as spiritual gifts. They need to realize there is nothing to be afraid of. Prayer and meditation can help them feel grounded. Connecting to a higher power can help them feel comforted, protected, and capable of accepting themselves.

Heightened Senses

Eighth house people have a heightened sensitivity to sound. Music can influence their emotional reactions. The pitch of people's voices, loudness of music, or sounds affect them greatly. The ability to hear subtle sounds or high pitch ringing is common; some believe these sounds come from the astral realm. This ability is often referred to as clairaudience which is the power to hear sounds that exist beyond the reach of ordinary experience. An example eighth house people share with me is when they hear someone call their name or hear the voice of a deceased loved one. Many twelfth house clients have shared with me that they have heard their name being called when they are alone. Sometimes it happens at night and they are woken up from a deep sleep in the middle of the night. This can be a scary experience but it only happens once in a while. Eighth house people share with me that these sounds often affect them when they are getting ready to go to sleep, when they are waking up, when they are concentrating, and when they are meditating. These experiences affect the auditory senses, and sometimes after hearing these high pitch sounds, they feel more sensitive to their environment. Their eardrums can still feel strange after these experiences. It often happens when they are alone; and sometimes when others are around they do not hear the same sounds the eighth house person does.

The belief in the afterlife, the power of the soul, and the belief in energy healing are all spiritual gifts eighth house people are attracted to. All of the psychic, unexplained experiences that eighth house people have are part of their journey, and are the blessings of having planets in this house.

All eighth house people have a spiritual gift. They just have to become more self-aware and practice trusting themselves. I have met a lot of people who had these types of experiences and sometimes they were not even aware of astrology.

After researching birth charts, I always found planets in the eighth or twelfth houses. Mystical and strange experiences are connected to both of these houses. Many experiences begin in childhood and many people block them. The unknown can be scary, and if the family did not nurture the psychic abilities we had when we were children, they might go dormant. There is a lot of research on children and how open they are to energy. As we grow older, we often lose touch with these spiritual gifts. Eighth house people need to embrace and awaken their abilities so they can help others in a powerful way. Eighth house people are learning to trust their abilities and should not doubt themselves. Listening to their intuition and gut instincts is crucial, especially when they are experiencing challenges in life. Eighth house people are meant to become spiritual. They can help awaken others to the spiritual side of life.

Chapter Ten

Depression, Anger, Anxiety, and Repression

Neptune is in my eighth house. I have always felt different even like an outcast. It's the deep, intense things that have always drawn me. It's considered taboo. It has been very difficult letting others get close to me and I have some trust and depression issues that I'm working through. You really blessed me with the bubble method because I was looking for alternatives to treat my depression without medication.
– Female, Europe

Eighth house people tend to hide emotions because they are very secretive and private people. They are mysterious, magnetic people. Scorpio is the natural ruler of the eighth house and is why eighth house people do not like to feel vulnerable. Having control over emotions and how others perceive them is important. Repressing emotions and refusing to feel them is an eighth house thing. Their emotions are so deep and powerful it is sometimes hard to embrace them, so they shut down. I call these behaviors "eighth house implosions" where they push down strong feelings and hold them inside until it continues to build.

For eighth house people, it's kind of like a boiling pot. They keep putting more things in the pot and it keeps boiling and stewing until eventually it boils over. Explosions of strong emotions are common for eighth house people. Eighth house people tend to repress their anger due to a secretive and private nature. When they stuff it down and refuse to allow themselves to feel it, they can become irritable and so intense that it's damaging to their physical body and health. Eighth house people often respond to stress by avoiding thinking or feeling things. Irritability, depression, and anxiety can manifest years later if they do not address underlying anger. Refusing to express themselves can lead to feelings of anger, depression, and anxiety.

To overcome these behaviors, eighth house people need to have a healthy outlet. It can be exercise, going for a long run, lifting weights, punching a bag or pillow, writing, or meditating. The important thing is to find something that works to relieve stress and get those pent-up feelings out of their physical body. Activities that can help them express those intense emotions will be beneficial.

Some eighth house people have shared with me that sex, working out, socializing, working towards a goal, and accomplishing things all help serve as an outlet for intense energy. The most important lesson to learn is how to practice taking care of themselves. Sometimes eighth house people don't know what to say and don't talk to anyone. They push people away when they are going through hard times. They might try to deny that anything is wrong and act like they are fine even if they're not.

Many eighth house people share with me that they suffer from depression off and on throughout their lives. Many things can trigger depression and feelings of loneliness. It could be a residue of years of denying their feelings, desires, wants and needs. Sacrificing themselves repeatedly for others can also be a trigger. Sometimes they are not sure how they will overcome unpleasant emotions. They might find it hard to get out of bed each day and get dressed. Sleep and diet might be affected. They often withdraw and hide and isolate themselves from people. Unhealthy coping can lead to further isolation.

Sometimes self-destructive behaviors are a way they try to cope. Eighth house people might start drinking more, overeating, abusing drugs and smoking. They might stop doing all the healthy activities that they normally do such as exercise, hanging out with friends, and pursuing hobbies. When they avoid all those healthy coping mechanisms, they can sometimes hit rock bottom. The good news is that there is a tiny fire inside them that kicks in, and it's the phoenix. The eighth house person is a survivor, surrounded by Scorpio energy, and snaps out of it suddenly and says to themselves, "Screw this. I am not going to lay here and feel sorry for myself anymore. I am going to get out of this bed and live. I am going to fight and get over this mess and never let anyone or anything bring me down." The survival instinct kicks in strongly for eighth house people and pushes them towards transformation. They can use their anger to keep surviving and it's that anger that helps them transform and overcome. Negative feelings help them face issues and return even stronger and braver than before. Another thing that happens is that their intuitive abilities grow more powerful after these rebirths and deaths.

Eighth house people have shared with me that they sometimes experience anxiety and panic attacks. It relates to what we discussed earlier about implosion and turning things onto oneself. If they are not expressing things outwardly then the energy is going to turn inward. They can eventually have trouble breathing and sometimes it is hard to know what triggers these attacks. It can happen when they feel relaxed or when they are trying to fall asleep. Panic attacks can strike at a time they least expected it, and this leaves them feeling out of control. Sometimes it happens because it's the first time they have been quiet and listened to their inner self and they are not distracted.

Eighth house people feel things deeply and they can't run and hide from those feelings. The cure is to feel. They must feel and let themselves experience negative emotions. Shutting down and shutting off is extreme and leads to all or nothing, black or white, love or hate absolutes which do not foster healing. This behavior can cause difficulties, and it can be beneficial to work with a counselor to process these intense experiences.

Eighth house people must realize that it is a positive thing to pursue counseling and have someone to discuss personal issues with. Eighth house people are used to everyone else telling them all their problems, and serve as counselors for everyone else, while they neglect their own needs. Eighth house people must realize it does not make them weak to get help, it's a strength. They can be role models for other eighth house people, friends, and family. Modeling healthy coping skills will help others around them realize they can also be more vulnerable.

Eighth house people want to appear strong. They do not want others to feel pity for them and that is one of their greatest fears. They want others to believe they have everything under control. The thing they need to remember is that they are human! Everyone has problems and no one is immune from difficult times. No one has a perfect life, and eighth house people need to realize that they are not meant to appear perfect and they can't control the unknown no matter how hard they try.

Issues such as anger, depression, and anxiety are those things that impact eighth house people throughout their lives. Healing and addressing the root cause of these feelings is important. Their health will be better and they can prevent disease. The thoughts and body are connected, and impact the physical body in many ways. Unresolved anger can be a vicious poison that affects the entire body and weakens the immune system.

Many eighth house people share with me that they struggle with sexual diseases and problems with the reproductive system as well as the gastrointestinal system. Since Scorpio rules the eighth house it makes sense that the bowels and elimination system are common issues. Many women share with me that they have experienced cysts of the ovaries, uterus, cervix, and problems with their menstrual cycles. I have the Moon, Chiron, and Jupiter all conjunct in the eighth house and I have several ovarian cysts and at one point they wanted to remove one of my ovaries. I also have fibroid tumors in my uterus that must be watched to ensure they don't grow. I have had my share of female reproductive health issues throughout my life. The first time I ever had a mammogram they found a hard lump and I had the scare of my life. I had to undergo a needle biopsy and thank God it was benign. I feel a lot of my health issues were linked to the repression of my pain and emotions. I realized that I would stuff my anger and never express it. I was never taught how to express anger and socialized to believe being angry was wrong. I now practice self-care and make time to write, journal, and communicate how I feel so I can get those feelings out of my physical body. I also accepted the fact that it's okay to be angry!

Many eighth house men have shared with me that they have problems with the prostate gland, tumors of the testicles, bowel problems, and constipation. Digestive problems are common with eighth house people. All those things that happened in the past that they did not heal or allow themselves to feel get backed up in the body. They can struggle with irritable bowel syndrome, constipation and stomach issues. They need to talk, express and release all their intense feelings. Processing their feelings is the key and is a direct link to their healing.

Repression of sexual urges is common for eighth house people. It is often all or nothing as far as intimacy goes, where they can have periods of an overabundant amount of intimacy or it's completely shut off. Sometimes it feels like being a monk or nun because the sex drive seems blocked. They can experience no desire at all. Repressing sexual urges is common for eighth house people and sometimes it is related to trauma. Many clients have shared experiences of being sexually abused or victimized. We will be discussing this area more in-depth in an upcoming chapter, but for now, it is important to realize that illness can manifest in the sexual organs due to unhealed trauma.

Eighth house people would benefit from bodywork, energy work, and any type of deep healing modality. Alternative medicine such as acupuncture can also help get to the root of health problems versus just taking medications that cover up the pain but never heal the deeper issue. Getting to the root cause of the real medical issue is the most important thing for eighth house people to do.

Eighth house people need to know that there is nothing to be ashamed of and they can talk about their problems. They do not always have to be the strong one and it's good to allow themselves to open up. Releasing past trauma and allowing healing to occur mentally, physically and spiritually will help eighth house people become greater healers themselves. Take one day at a time and practice.

Chapter Eleven

Other People's Resources, Inheritances, and Sacrifice

In some ways suffering ceases to be suffering at the moment it finds a meaning, such as the meaning of a sacrifice.
– Viktor E. Frankl

When astrologers discuss the eighth house, they call it the house of death. Anything associated with the goods of the dead such as wills, land, estates, and life insurance plans are related to this area of life. When I first started researching this house, I was fascinated by its mystery and depth. Based on my personal experiences, I came to draw my own opinions and feelings about this house. I realized that there are blessings that come from other people when planets are in this house, and it is all about destiny and greater growth of the soul. I will discuss what I have seen with clients with eighth house planets and how they benefited through the resources of others in unique ways.

First, let's discuss career fields and how eighth house people are attracted to certain jobs and professions. Many eighth house people end up working in careers such as finance, banking, stock market, real estate and accounting. I have done a lot of charts for eighth house people and many naturally were involved in these types of careers where they were taking care of other people's money in some way. They had good luck in these types of career fields and felt they stumbled upon them by chance. Some felt content but others reported feeling something was missing in their work. It really depends on which planets are in the eighth to get a better perspective.

The eighth house is related to inheritance, and financial gain often comes through the mother or father's side of the family depending on which planets are placed here. Sometimes inheritances come through grandparents, uncles, aunts, and spouses. For instance, if the Sun is in the eighth house, benefits come from the father or his side of the family. Sometimes the paternal grandparents help financially and support the family. One client explained to me that as a Sun in the eighth house person, she never understood why her paternal grandfather paid for her entire college and even helped her financially when she attended college. She never really saw this connection until she realized she had an eighth house Sun and learned about other people's money.

The second house is the opposite house from the eighth and it relates to money, earnings, security and saving for your own future. The eighth on the other hand is connected to money that comes from someone else such as an intimate partner, spouse or family member. Looking at financial benefits that come from outside your own earnings is eighth house energy. Money coming from your own hard work is related to the second house. An example is a client of mine who had the Moon in the eighth house and she did benefit financially from her maternal grandmother and she also inherited psychic abilities from her. Spiritual gifts are also considered "inheritances" and they do not always manifest as money, land or property. Many times, they can be gifts of intuition, dreaming, writing abilities, intellectual abilities, and even artistic abilities.

From personal experience doing consultations, I have noticed that other people often sacrifice things for eighth house people. Clients have always validated my research by sharing with me specific examples of how people have blessed them financially and emotionally. This is one of the positive areas of the eighth house and is often overlooked.

Sacrifice is giving up or letting go of something important in order to help others. Self-sacrifice is often associated with the eighth house as well, but it does not necessarily represent a negative experience. Sacrifice can be an amazing act of love and a part of spiritual development. Sometimes eighth house people feel that they naturally let go and give up their happiness and security for others. Some eighth house people feel they have a heavy burden to carry when it comes to helping others. The eighth house indeed encourages us to heal and grow stronger as a person. Eighth house people will experience a time where they have to let go of something or someone they love. It might be a relationship partner, friend, or family member who keeps hurting them and is unhealthy. It could be an abusive relationship, or needing to release coworkers who do not appreciate them and only take advantage of them. The reason eighth house sacrifice can be painful is because of connections with people. Having a deep connection and having to release it is what makes it difficult. If eighth house people were not deep individuals and incapable of connecting on a soul level, then these sacrifices would not be as difficult. Because they are meant to feel intense, powerful emotions, part of the eighth house journey is to feel extremes in happiness and unhappiness.

Many eighth house people feel they must sacrifice their sexual desires and needs for their partner. They rarely feel that their partner can satisfy their emotional or physical needs. They have high expectations of others and expect others to be on their high-intensity level. The truth is that most people are not capable of feeling the same way an eighth house person does.

Through sacrifice, eighth house people transform and heal. Sacrifice helps them appreciate the wonderful blessings in their lives. It is important to see sacrifice as something positive that will create strength and shift the belief that they are losing something. Sometimes it's unconscious and they don't even realize they are sacrificing, it just happens. They develop patterns of behavior and get comfortable hiding what they want. Giving up something for loved ones or to help others is a talent and eighth house people do it well. Later in life, eighth house people start attracting all the things they want and desire. Their lives often get better with age. As they grow older all their dreams start to come true and they feel more inner contentment. It is important for eight house people to forgive themselves for mistakes and release all the guilt from the past that relates to sacrifice.

Chapter Twelve

Trauma and Self-Care

That which is to give light must endure burning.
– Viktor E. Frankl

What is Trauma?

Trauma is experiencing a disturbing or distressing situation or event. There are three main types of traumas: acute, chronic, and complex. Acute trauma results from a single incident such as a car accident. Chronic trauma is often repeated and prolonged by stress such as domestic violence, childhood abuse, fighting in war, or witnessing violence. Being exposed to multiple traumatic events that are interpersonal in nature is called complex trauma. Many people with planets in the eighth house experience trauma. It can be an emotional scar that affects them psychologically, physically, and spiritually. Trauma affects everyone differently and each person has a unique way to cope, adjust, and heal after difficult experiences. After experiencing trauma, it is normal to experience flashbacks, depression, anger, anxiety, and other uncomfortable experiences. Trauma events involve three main areas: hyperarousal, reexperiencing, and avoidance/numbing. An exaggerated startle reflex, difficulty concentrating, impulsivity, and anxiety are part of hyperarousal. Having flashbacks, nightmares, increased perception of a threat, uncomfortable thoughts, emotions, and physical sensations are all part of reexperiencing. Avoidance and numbing involve diminished interest in activities and detaching from the physical body (*The Body Keeps the Score*, Bessel Van der Kolk, MD).

A tool psychologists, social workers and counselors use to access trauma in childhood before the age of 18 and analyze how it impacts us when we are adults is called the Adverse

Childhood Experiences (ACEs) assessment. This assessment shows the impact our childhood experiences had on us. You can find this questionnaire online to download it for free.

There are 10 specific questions and you want to answer Yes or No to the below:

1. Did you feel that you didn't have enough to eat, had to wear dirty clothes, or had no one to protect or take care of you?

2. Did you lose a parent through divorce, abandonment, death, or other reason?

3. Did you live with anyone who was depressed, mentally ill, or attempted suicide?

4. Did you live with anyone who had a problem with drinking or using drugs, including prescription drugs?

5. Did your parents or adults in your home ever hit, punch, beat, or threaten to harm each other?

6. Did you live with anyone who went to jail or prison?

7. Did a parent or adult in your home ever swear at you, insult you, or put you down?

8. Did a parent or adult in your home ever hit, beat, kick, or physically hurt you in any way?

9. Did you feel that no one in your family loved you or thought you were special?

10. Did you experience unwanted sexual contact (such as fondling or oral/anal/vaginal intercourse/penetration)?

Trauma impacts us even if we don't realize it. If you answered "yes" to 1-3 questions you are at intermediate risk for toxic stress. Four or more confirmed experiences will show that you are at high risk for toxic stress. Toxic stress is linked to a higher incidence of health problems such as cardiovascular diseases, stroke, pulmonary diseases, asthma, diabetes, and obesity. Unhealed trauma that we experience in childhood affects us well into adulthood. Many eighth house people have experienced four or more of the above during childhood. These experiences molded the person they are today making them more resilient. Eighth house people need to ask themselves how they survived. What was special about them that enabled them to overcome these difficult situations? I believe it's inborn resilience and strength. They had to be strong to survive the above types of experiences. There were personality traits that were utilized to help them succeed and heal from the past. Children who have eighth house planets as adults transform, regenerate, and allow themselves to be reborn. They embrace the newness of change and push forward towards the future. They are survivors. I always recommend to eighth house people to see a therapist and work on addressing anything in childhood that still holds them back. Counseling and psychotherapy fields interest eighth house people and many of them are natural at helping others, and even become therapists themselves. They need to let go of their need for control and allow themselves to seek help if it's needed.

Below are some tips for healing trauma and understanding its impact on health.

Types of Traumas
There are many things that can be traumatic that most people do not think about. The following are traumas that we often invalidate and ignore.

- Neglect
- Having a loved one with severe mental illness or special needs
- Experiencing multiple losses in a row
- Chronic Pain
- Abuse from authority figures
- Burnout
- Infertility
- Bullying
- Infidelity
- Experiencing forms of oppression
- Poverty and unemployment

Body Awareness
Knowing yourself and understanding how trauma affects your life and health is important. When you understand how traumatic experiences have impacted your life and recognize behaviors, emotions, and patterns then you can have greater power in managing them. The best way to heal trauma is to find a professional such as a trauma counselor, therapist, energy healer, or even massage therapist to begin the recovery process. Finding a trusted confidant who you can be vulnerable with and feel comfortable sharing emotions with is the number one thing that helps people heal from trauma. Other things that help people heal from trauma include grounding exercises, self-reflection, relaxation, yoga, meditation, diaphragmatic breathing, and muscle tension exercises.

The first step in healing trauma is to become aware of your own physical body. It is important to understand where you carry stress and tension. Dr. Bessel Van der Kolk, trauma specialist, calls this skill Body Scanning or the "wet noodle concept". This method involves self-regulation. Self-regulation activities used for treating trauma are body scanning, diaphragmatic breathing, peripheral vision exercises, and pelvic floor exercises. Body scanning is a head-to-toe awareness of tensed muscles and implementing ways to relax them. Tightening muscles for five seconds and releasing them is part of this technique. Breathing deeply in and holding for a few seconds and then breathing out releasing tension during the head-to-toe scan will foster greater relaxation and calmness. When we are relaxed, we are not in the fight or flight mode or hyperarousal mode of survival. Feeling safe and secure increases feelings of comfort, safety, and security. Being in this state physically helps the body heal and process past experiences.

Peripheral vision exercises involve concentration and focus. They can help in healing trauma. Focus on a spot straight ahead of you. Slowly keeping your focus continue to widen your field of view and notice what you see in your peripheral vision which is on each side of your view. Trauma treatments like Eye Movement Desensitization and Reprocessing (EMDR) have been found to be successful in helping trauma victims remember, process, and release painful memories. EMDR with a trained therapist is similar to this basic exercise below and helps the body relax. Another technique to reduce muscle tension is pelvic floor relaxation which involves lying on the floor tensing the four points and muscles in the pelvis, and then releasing them. Ensure you breathe deeply holding the breath and then releasing the breath while tightening these muscles. Whenever you feel clenching or tightening of your muscles you can stop and find a place to practice these basic techniques. This will put your body in a state of awareness that will help with self-regulation.

5-4-3-2-1 Technique (From TherapistAid.com)

This technique helps you get in touch with your senses and notice small details that your mind typically tunes out. Below is the technique you can use on yourself when you feel overwhelmed with emotions, intrusive thoughts, and unpleasant memories. You have control over what you are experiencing and can utilize this technique to gain greater focus.

What are 5 things that you can see? Look for small details such as a pattern on the ceiling, the way light reflects off a surface, or an object you never noticed.

What are 4 things you can feel? Notice the sensation of clothing on your body, the sun on your skin, or the feelings of the chair you are sitting in. Pick up an object and examine its weight, texture, and other physical qualities.

What are 3 things that you can hear? Pay special attention to the sounds your mind has tuned out, such as a ticking clock, distant traffic, or trees blowing in the wind.

What are 2 things you can smell? Try to notice smells in the air around you, like an air freshener or freshly mowed grass. You may also look around for something that has a scent, such as a flower or a candle.

What is 1 thing you can taste? Carry gum, candy, or small snacks for this step. Pop one in your mouth and focus your attention closely on the flavors.

Grounding

Grounding techniques can be a helpful way to manage your stress, unpleasant feelings, and traumatic memories. Grounding techniques help control symptoms by turning your attention away from unpleasant thoughts, memories, or worries, and refocusing on the present moment. Grounding means reconnecting to the physical body and to the earth. The purpose of grounding techniques is to encourage a healthy way for trauma survivors to step away from negative thoughts, feelings, or flashbacks. It helps you focus on what is in front of you in the present moment and environment. Below is an example of a grounding meditation you can use to connect to the earth and replenish your energy. This grounding technique was shared with me from my friend and can be found on YouTube and online.

Grounding Exercise:
The Tree of Life Meditation Technique

1. Sit in a quiet spot.
2. Sit in the lotus position or whatever position that is most comfortable for you. Ensure your spine is straight.
3. Imagine yourself as a tree.
4. Imagine above you are rising into the sky branches of that tree. This is where you will draw energy from the Divine Father.
5. Imagine below you are going down into Mother Earth, to the root system of that tree. This is where you will draw energy from Divine Mother.
6. Now you will start the process of breathing in divine energy. Breathe in through your nose and out through your mouth.
7. First imagine and feel pulling in or breathing in energy through the branch system (Divine Father) into your physical body and aura. When you breathe in this energy, imagine that it replaces something unwanted. When you breathe out, imagine all this unwanted material going out of your body. Do this until you feel that this system is functioning well and feels balanced.
8. Now imagine and feel pulling in or breathing in energy through the root system (Divine Mother) into your physical body and aura. When you breathe in this energy, imagine that it replaces something unwanted. When you breathe out, imagine all this unwanted material going out. Do this until you feel that this system is functioning well and feels balanced.
9. Now imagine and feel pulling in energy from both the branch systems (Divine Father) and the root system (Divine Mother) at the same time. Energy will be flowing in from both systems at the same time into your

body. When you breathe in this energy, imagine that it replaces something unwanted. When you breathe out, imagine all this unwanted material going out.

10. Repeat this process of breathing in energy from both systems and then expelling all the unwanted material out as you breathe out. Continue this until you feel balanced and fully energized.

11. Use large circular breaths when breathing in and out. Connect the inhale with the exhale like a smoothly turning wheel. Follow the rhythm and pace that feels right for your body.

12. Finally, when breathing in both energies, feel them uniting in your heart and giving love. As you breathe out, send love out to your family, friends, animals, planets, and all people. Feel love everywhere surrounding you outside and inside because you are one with everything.

Another activity that can help connect you to your physical body is called Body Awareness. This activity brings you in the here and now by helping you focus on sensations in the body. Recognize what you feel during each of the below steps. It would be beneficial to journal your experiences with these exercises to gain greater self-awareness.

Body Awareness Technique

1. Take 5 long, deep breaths through your nose and exhale through puckered lips.

2. Place both feet flat on the floor. Wiggle your toes. Curl and uncurl your toes several times. Spend a moment noticing the sensations in your feet.

3. Stomp your feet on the ground several times. Pay attention to the sensations in your feet and legs as you contact the ground.

4. Clench your hands into fists, then release the tension. Repeat this 10 times.

5. Press your palms together. Press them harder and hold this pose for 15 seconds. Pay attention to the feeling of tension in your hands and arms.

6. Rub your palms together briskly. Notice the sound and the feeling of warmth.

7. Reach your hands over your head like you're trying to reach the sky. Stretch like this for 5 seconds. Bring your arms down and let them relax at your sides.

8. Take 5 more deep breaths and notice the feeling of calm in your body.

What is Self-Care?

Self-care involves taking time to replenish our own energy. Focusing on taking care of your body, mind, and spirit balances many areas of life. I like the saying, "You can't pour from an empty cup." This means you must fill your own cup first, replenish your own energy and give yourself time to recharge. Reflecting on daily activities and slowing down to truly focus on feelings will help balance all areas of life. Examples of self-care are meditation, yoga, deep breathing, getting a massage, spending time alone, doing something creative, setting boundaries, working on hobbies, listening to music, journaling, hiking, exercising, being in nature, cuddling with pets, and spending time outdoors.

Self-care works differently for eighth house people depending on your Sun Sign. Those with similar energies and shared elements will benefit from similar activities. For example, I find that many people who experience difficulties meditating and silencing their minds are often air signs. They will find physical movement and mental activities that challenge their brain to be more effective. Earth signs such as Taurus and Virgo will benefit by being outdoors, breathing fresh air, working in the garden, and feeling the earth beneath their feet.

The Elements & Self-Care

Water Signs: Cancer, Scorpio, Pisces – The Feelers

The water signs can utilize self-care techniques that are more calming and address the spiritual pillar. They benefit through contemplation, prayer, meditation, breathing exercises, quiet time, listening to music and journaling feelings. Water signs will enjoy self-reflection, time by themselves and focusing on emotional expression. Water signs traditionally benefit from textbook self-care activities like mindfulness. Mindfulness is being in the present moment and allowing yourself to experience the now. Water signs benefit by doing creative and spiritual activities to reduce stress.

Earth Signs: Virgo, Capricorn, Taurus – The Planners

The earth signs can utilize self-care techniques that are more practical and address the physical pillar. They may find meditation and mindfulness exercises more difficult. Earth signs benefit by spending time in nature, walking outdoors, being near water and working in the garden. Planning events and working on tasks for the future are comforting. Focusing on accomplishing goals or finishing projects reduces stress. Working on hobbies and completing tasks might be easier for earth signs to implement into their self-care schedule. Earth signs like doing self-care activities that are practical, organized, and planned.

Air Signs: Gemini, Libra, Aquarius – The Thinkers

The air signs can utilize self-care techniques that are intellectually stimulating and address the mental pillar. Air signs find it difficult to quiet and still their active minds. Traditional self-care techniques may be challenging for these signs. They should focus on self-care techniques such as reading, writing, and teaching someone a new skill. Sitting still and trying to meditate might cause more stress and increase overthinking. Playing games, debating topics, challenging the mind with crossword puzzles, and doing something fun will benefit them. The air signs like doing self-care activities that involve the mind, and social activities.

Fire Signs: Leo, Sagittarius, Aries – The Doers

The fire signs can utilize self-care techniques that are action-oriented addressing the emotional pillar. Fire signs like a challenge and can benefit by competition, playing sports, exercising, traveling, being outdoors, and moving around. Doing something physical and strenuous works for them. Self-care activities can't be boring. Involving other people and socializing is helpful. They recharge by doing something that requires movement and that brings them happiness. The fire signs like doing self-care activities that are hands-on.

It is important to understand which self-care activities help you unwind, relax, and feel better. Try different things and make time for healthy activities. Develop a self-care plan and list all the things you enjoy doing. Write down your plan and start implementing at least one self-care activity daily into your routine. Start small and develop a routine that you can stick with. You can naturally build upon your plan and add more activities. The key is to start somewhere and make the first steps towards taking care of yourself. You will be more equipped at helping others when you feel energized, happy, healthy, and calm.

Chapter Thirteen

Planets in the Eighth & Transits through the Eighth

Sun in the Eighth

The Sun in the eighth house is a powerful placement. The Sun represents the outer appearance and your main identity. It shows where you shine and how you reveal yourself to the world. Having the Sun in the eighth house intensifies Scorpio energy and personality traits. This placement creates a secretive person who is very private. Hiding things from others and avoiding telling anyone your secrets comes naturally. This is a mysterious placement and people are interested in getting to know you. People are extremely attracted to your energy. Magnetic and attractive, your presence is powerful and people notice you. The Sun here opens up all the dark secrets and taboo things about the eighth house. You can bring hidden things to the surface, exposing other people's secrets. Born with natural psychic abilities and strong intuition, you are able to see through people's true motives. Empathic, you can feel other people's energy easily and notice everything that is happening in the environment. Your spiritual gift is perception and it enables you to know people's true thoughts and feelings. This heightened psychic sensitivity attracts anything secret or taboo and brings it into your conscious awareness.

When the Sun is placed here it creates an interest in astrology, mysticism, numerology, ghosts, and anything occult, deep, and transforming. There can be a controlling nature and a desire for power. The astrological sign the Sun is placed in can affect the expression of these energies. For instance, if you are a Capricorn then you might be practical, realistic and scrutinize anything that is mystical and are more cautious about trusting your psychic abilities. One of the main things with this placement is there is a natural spiritual gift. You can benefit from the father or the father's side of the family. There is often some type of inheritance which could be money, property, land, or even a psychic ability. An example could be that you dream about future events and find out that your grandfather had the same ability. A paternal grandparent could have helped you financially in your early years to make sure you had a better life. Sacrifices other people make for you involve material blessings. Benefits come from the sacrifices of others.

You are an intense person and people who need healing are drawn into your life. Other people readily share their personal problems, divulging their deep secrets. You are a great listener and natural born counselor. Sun in the eighth people make excellent therapists, psychologists, detectives, researchers, and energy healers. Blessed with natural perceptive, intuitive and psychic abilities you seem to know what to say to others in their time of need. There are darker energies that can come with this placement such as greed, jealousy, anger, and a need for power. The goal is to use your spiritual gifts to help others and learn to become a more trusting person. Studying the mysteries of the universe will bring happiness and contentment.

Eighth house people are wounded healers who experience a lot of transformations, deaths and rebirths triggering personality changes. Change is a constant challenge that makes you stronger. You transform and regenerate just like the mythical phoenix bird, dying and being reborn. The most important thing to remember about this placement is learning to trust your intuition. Through changing and adapting you recognize your true nature as a soul sent here to earth for a special mission and purpose.

Moon in the Eighth

When the Moon is placed in the eighth house, you are a person born with a highly sensitive emotional nature. You are drawn to anything mysterious and fascinated by hidden things. Your emotional nature is intense and secretive. Hiding your true emotions and feelings from others due to fears of being misunderstood is a way to protect yourself. Emotionally you experience extremes, such as love and hate, black and white, and trust or distrust. Early in life you were fascinated with death and sometimes terrified of it. You are connected to spirits and often see ghosts as a child. Attracted to anything that is unexplained such as UFOs, aliens, spirits, psychic abilities, and mysteries. Understanding death on a core level is heightened because you are born intuitive. You may have laid in bed at night and thought, "What if I die? What will happen to me, my soul?" Worried about losing loved ones you may have been afraid of dying as a child.

You feel different than others because you are born with a complex emotional nature. You feel lonely even among friends and family. You can feel lonely because you have special psychic abilities that can manifest themselves through your dreams, intuition, gut instinct, and visions. You need to learn to trust your perceptions in order to give insight to others. Intuition protects you from harm and enables you to avoid being hurt.

Attracting people with emotional pain is common with this placement. Your energy draws individuals into your life that need healing and who have wounds. These individuals are not always good for your life. Remember it is not your responsibility to take on the karma of others or try to fix them. You are not responsible for healing the entire world but need to utilize your spiritual abilities. Be careful not to drain your energy or take on other people's pain making it your own. Absorbing everything in the environment can cause health problems, suffering, depression and negativity if you allow these lower-level energies into your life. Your energy vibrates at a high level and protecting yourself energetically creates strength. Visualizing a ball of yellow light surrounding you when you are in large groups will help you find protection.

Sometimes you feel that others dislike you and this is because you can see through people to the core of their being. Picking up other people's true feelings can cause tremendous emotional pain and sadness. Other people are not aware of their motivations, subconscious thoughts, or body language but you notice these things. You are born with an antenna that picks up all the hidden, secretive and taboo things in the environment. You will benefit greatly from meditation and relaxation. Journaling thoughts, feelings and perceptions can bring emotional comfort.

You can struggle with emotional highs and lows. You might feel that people are always hurting or taking advantage of you. Learning to have boundaries with others and control your sensitive nature will help balance these negative experiences. At some time in your life, you will feel victimized by others sexually, financially, or emotionally. Your wound revolves around trust and intimacy issues. When you have sexual intercourse with someone you merge with that person on a spiritual level and it can hard for you to let them go. Suffering comes from relationships and sometimes others take advantage of you. Feeling betrayed by those you trust is a spiritual lesson. It is important to realize these experiences are part of the eighth house journey. You are meant to become a stronger person because of them. You are a survivor and have great healing strength and abilities. Even if you suffer and hit rock bottom you will rise up like the phoenix out of the ashes. Regeneration and healing are a blessing with the Moon placed here. You may cry yourself to sleep, depressed, lost, and tired, but eventually the warrior comes out. An inner strength lives inside you. No matter how low you feel, an inner voice tells you to rise up. This makes you stronger, healthier and happier.

You are a natural healer and are often drawn to careers that delve deeply into other people's lives. You enjoy bringing the unconscious to conscious awareness. You excel in careers such as psychiatry, counseling, therapy, psychology, medicine, research, criminal work, detective work, coroner, mortuary director, and any metaphysical field. You have healing hands and benefit from studying Reiki, Pranic healing, and healing touch modalities. Working with energy and sending energy to others is something you might naturally be good at.

You may have lost your mother at a young age through unexpected death or your mother might be very controlling and possessive. Your relationship with your mother is intense and teaches you a lot about trust. You will inherit something from your mother or her side of the family. Inheriting land, property, possessions, money, or psychic abilities is a common eighth house experience. Spiritual gifts come from your mother's side of the family such as a maternal grandmother or grandfather. Benefits come from females, and other people sacrifice things for your life to be better. Your financial success and material comfort will almost always come to you from someone else such as family, friends or your marriage partner.

Embrace the blessings that come your way. The Moon in the eighth house is a blessing and a curse. The blessing is that you will be a true healer and able to serve others in a deep way. The curse is that you feel a lack of depth in your relationships and feel that no one understands you. You get bored easily with others if they cannot hold the level of intensity that you need. You can become restless throughout your life. Looking for your "soul-mate" and deep intimacy becomes almost obsessive. Intimate partners lack something you need. You connect to others through sex and deep emotional interactions. Your emotional happiness is dependent upon being able to connect deeply with people. You need to realize that your feelings of loneliness will lessen once you begin to see your oneness with others and not your separateness. You are a true healer and need to use your gifts to help others heal and transform themselves.

Through healing others, you heal yourself.

Venus in the Eighth

When Venus is placed in the eighth house, you are focused on keeping your love nature secret and private. You will benefit through the marriage partner and tend to marry someone of a higher financial status than yourself. Blessings come through romantic partners. Your love nature is deep, possessive, and intense. When you fall in love you don't take it lightly. Intimacy and trust are crucial in order for you to feel comfortable with a partner. Before you can become sexually active with a partner, you will wait until they gain your trust. You struggle with trusting others and find it difficult to show vulnerability with your partner. Before sharing intimate feelings, you will want to know how others feel. You can feel insecure at times because of being afraid of being hurt. Relationships are all or nothing for you. A high level of commitment and loyalty from your partner is needed and expected. You can become jealous, vengeful, and aggressive if you feel mistreated or betrayed.

Secretive individuals are attractive as well as those who work behind the scenes in some way. The partners you attract are often involved with law enforcement, detective work, psychiatry, counseling, and career fields where psychological depth is involved. You are attracted to intense and passionate individuals. In relationships you are passionate and possessive of your partner. You expect a high level of depth in your relationship and if you do not experience that you will cut ties. You feel most relationships are superficial and prefer to be alone. You cannot tolerate superficiality in your intimate relationships and are not a casual dater. You enjoy a one-on-one relationship that is stable and serious. Marrying someone solely based on their financial status is common with this placement. You are attracted to people who have money, wealth, and status. If a partner struggles financially, it will turn you off, even if you love them. Be cautious about marrying someone solely based on their financial success and wealth. Chemistry and attraction are also important aspects of a long-lasting relationship.

You attract partners that are wounded in some way. Falling in love with others comes easily if you feel needed. Be careful and think about the differences between love and pity. Sometimes you can believe that you are in love but it's actually your own intuitive ability of feeling others' pain. Connecting to others' pain often brings you a partner that is unstable, unhealthy or unreliable. You may learn this the hard way and feel victimized at some time in your life. Sex and love go hand and hand which requires a deep emotional connection. Sacrificing your own feelings for others and avoiding red flags in relationships can bring heartache. When you have sex with a partner you develop a strong attachment and bond that can be difficult to break. Be cautious about who you share intimacy with because you can feel taken advantage of. You need emotional depth in your relationships in order to find fulfillment and happiness.

Mars in the Eighth

When Mars is placed in the eighth house, you are a person who has a strong sexual nature. You often find yourself involved in relationships that are deep and highly sexual. Bonding with someone on a physical level makes it difficult to ever let go of that person. You become jealous, angry, obsessive and find yourself drawn to intense, unhealthy relationships. You enjoy pushing people to the breaking point and can be reckless in your dealings with others. Temper flare-ups and emotional outbursts are common. Living on the edge, seeking an adrenaline rush through speeding, skydiving, and risky behavior can lead to accidents. You are an intensely passionate person who experiences dramatic shifts in emotion although you try to repress them. There is a need to control your intense feelings and keep things hidden from others. You can be fiercely private and reclusive when you feel vulnerable. On the other hand you can lash out at others in a fiery rage of anger.

Exercising regularly and having a physical outlet for all of your intense energy will help balance emotions. Repressing your emotions, sexual urges, and desires can make you vulnerable to illness. Avoiding extremes and finding a healthy balance should be part of your self-care plan. You're known for restricting yourself of things or overindulging in them because you are an "all or nothing" type of person.

Intuitive, insightful, perceptive and blessed with a strong imagination you have a gift for digging up secrets. You can excel in police or detective work where you can serve behind the scenes in some way. You have an inquisitive mind and an eye for detail. Researching and delving deeply into topics that require investigative skills suit your personality. People are drawn to you and like to share their problems. To process your complex emotional nature, you need alone time. Experiencing conflicts with family over inheritances, land, wills, and the material resources of someone close to you is common. There can be challenges with the marriage partner. You may inherit money from your father, grandfather or through a male family member. You might have to battle to claim what was given to you or may be cut out of someone's will because of your aggressive behavior.

You can have special talents and are attracted to the healing fields such as medicine, massage therapy, psychology, and any field dealing with other people's resources. If you do not feel deeply connected with others or if you are not able to dig deeply into situations, you can become bored and restless. You are sensitive to other people's emotions, especially anger, rage, jealousy and resentment. With practice and time, you can become a powerful force of change in the lives of others.

Mercury in the Eighth

When Mercury is placed in the eighth house, you are a person who hides their thoughts and ideas from others. It is difficult for you to trust someone because you are a very private person. Blessed with a perceptive mind seeing through fakeness, superficiality, and verbal accolades is a gift. There is a need for conversation that's deep and meaningful. You enjoy probing the minds of others and enjoy trying to figure out if others are telling you the truth. Mental games and exercises strengthen the mind. Mental connections lead to greater emotional connections.

Born as an imaginative thinker, you excel by diving deep into complex subjects and solving problems. Understanding how things work on a deeper level brings comfort. Your mind is like a sponge absorbing everything going on in the environment. This ability can lead to confusion, irritability, and depression. You pick up other people's thoughts easily and it's hard to differentiate your own thoughts. Psychically gifted, you might have the ability to read minds, although you may not even realize it. Gifted with listening to others you are able to help others who have problems to share. Others like to discuss their secrets and similar spiritual interests with you. You enjoy talking with others about important life matters such as life, death, love, finances, and property.

You make an excellent psychologist or counselor. You have communication abilities that pull out the truth in others. Sensing what is going on with others, you are able to verbalize the words they need to hear. Your gift of expression touches others on a deep emotional level. If you like someone you may never tell them directly. Internalizing your anger can lead to explosions where you use your sharp tongue and lash out at others. Writing down your intense thoughts and ideas in a journal would be beneficial. Writing is a good stress reliever.

Enjoyment comes through reading detective books, mystery novels, and metaphysical books on topics such as astrology, tarot, numerology, and healing. It is important to discuss spiritual topics with people who are trusted and who challenge your belief system. You would benefit by studying the paranormal and researching mystical phenomena.

Jupiter in the Eighth

When Jupiter is in the eighth house, you are a person blessed with generosity and good fortune. Out of all the placements in the eighth house, having Jupiter here is the most beneficial. Others will take care of you financially, materially, and emotionally. Inheritances that come through property, wills, possessions, or special spiritual gifts are passed down to you from family members. Blessings come from the sacrifices others make for you and they will give up things in their own life to ensure that you succeed. Blessings come from those closest to you. Jupiter is all about abundance and this placement protects you from the harsher eighth house energies.

Many blessings are bestowed upon you and it's best to overcome any feelings of guilt. Accept that you are destined to benefit from others' generosity. You may be the person who has to sacrifice things in your own life at some time for those you care about. Give up things that are unhealthy, especially behaviors, emotions, thoughts, and things that are not helping you grow. When you release things then the universe will bless you with more. Your greatest dreams and wishes will start to come true. Letting go of the old helps you grow. Pain and heartache push you to the limit. As soon as you truly let things go, release things, allow yourself to move on, blessings will arrive. You will receive an answer, a gift, or a special present from the universe.

This placement is very powerful because you are born with psychic abilities. You might have clairvoyant dreams, see the future, or you may be able to sense other people's motives. It's important to share your spiritual gifts with the world. The more you share your insights the more you grow spiritually. You are lucky because you will always feel there is something outside yourself guarding you, watching you, and protecting you. Angels, spirit guides, deceased loved ones are always surrounding you.

Saturn in the Eighth

When Saturn is in the eighth house, repressing emotions and a strong secretive nature is common. You work hard to avoid change. Controlling by nature, you dislike the unexpected. Even though you have psychic abilities and a strong intuition about things, you can be afraid of trusting yourself. Don't repress your natural healing gifts and sensitive nature. Learn to be more expressive. Serious at heart, you worry about security and losing those you love. You may be afraid of death and experience loss at an early age. This experience changes you on a deep level and can cause insecurities.

Benefits come by embracing change and learning to trust others. Reading books about change, growth, and preparing for the future can help you adapt. Repressing emotions and sexual urges can lead to health problems. You may be afraid of having sexual intimacy and have rigid attitudes about it. Sharing anything intimate with others makes you feel uncomfortable because you are afraid of being hurt. It is difficult for you to communicate deeply with others or even know how to speak at times. Learning to face your fears is the karmic lesson of this placement. Feeling responsible for other people's actions, it's difficult for you to understand why people do the things they do. You have high expectations and expect others to be as responsible as you are. Because of the wall you put up around yourself, people can perceive you as cold or unloving. The fact is you are a loving person even if you don't know how to show it outwardly. Taking care of others' practical needs is easier than displaying emotional support. Restricting yourself too much can impact your ability to experience happiness. Let your hair down sometimes, and learn to have more fun!

You may have a karmic debt to balance out regarding other people's finances. If you inherit money, you may be blocked from receiving it in some way or others might take what was rightfully yours. Other people's resources will be a source of confusion in your life. Being placed in a position where you have to take responsibility for someone else's property, business, finances, medical bills, and retirement plans tests your strength. Making practical decisions and being the responsible person who makes sure that everyone is financially taken care of comes naturally. You need to try to see these life experiences as gifts and not burdens.

Uranus in the Eighth

When Uranus is placed in the eighth house, you find freedom of expression by studying the occult. Associating yourself with everything taboo brings excitement. The mystical side of life fascinates you and you are born with an interest in anything unique or different. Embracing change while feeling free to express yourself fully brings happiness. It is common to experience transformation and it seems like your entire personality is constantly reborn. Waking up and feeling like you are not the same person anymore happens unexpectedly. Uranus energy is electric, unexpected, and shocking so you are not always aware of when a transformation will take place.

There can be electric attractions and your sense of sexual identity can be unique. You are someone who does not like labels and will rebel against traditional sex roles. Gender might not mean the same thing to you as it does to others. You always test the boundaries of how far you can expand your creative and eccentric mind.

Experiencing vivid dreams, astral projection, déjà vu, and out of body experiences can happen in childhood. Unexpected psychic visions and auditory sounds come into your awareness out of the blue. Writing down your perceptions and visions is important because helping others is part of your mission. Experiencing the unexpected death of a family member, friend or someone close to you is common. Traumatic situations can happen unexpectedly and can take time to heal.

Financial benefits come through your marriage partner or immediate family. Other people play a big role in your material and financial success. Things like inheriting money unexpectedly or property can drastically change your life and livelihood. Change is a constant energy and by embracing it you will find greater happiness.

Be careful about reckless behavior and doing things without thinking. Taking unnecessary risks just to feel adrenaline pumping through your veins makes you feel alive. Being bored, stagnant, or trapped makes you feel like breaking free. You enjoy experiencing dangerous situations because you like to push the limits. Take caution while driving and watch speeding. You need to be careful around knives and anything that is sharp. Accidents happens when you are rushing or forcing change too quickly. It is important to feel that you have control over your life and can make your own decisions. Settling down and focusing on goals can prevent many unforeseen misfortunes. Take care of your health, family, friends and responsibilities, and avoid taking needless risks.

Neptune in the Eighth

Neptune in the eighth house heightens a highly sensitive and emotional nature. You are compassionate and feel others' pain easily. Born with a strong imagination there is the potential to have visions of a spiritual nature. Experiencing strange fantasies is common and you are very interested in psychic phenomenon. There is an inner belief in a higher power and faith in something greater than yourself that helps you overcome suffering. There could be fears about supernatural forces, although you can't resist studying about them. Learning as much as possible about the spiritual world will bring comfort. You want to understand the soul and what happens after you die. You might suffer emotionally and feel lonely. Abandonment issues can make it difficult to trust others. You may feel like no one understands you and this increases your need to withdraw from others and remain secretive. There is a chance that you will have powerful dreams. Writing down your dreams is important as they can be used as a guide in your waking life.

You can feel wounded by someone you trusted. Feeling victimized emotionally, mentally, physically, or sexually can cause pain. Sexuality is a subject that fascinates you as well as brings you heartache. Seeking a soul mate and someone who is mystical can lead you down a rabbit hole. Seeing people with rose-colored glasses can lead to disappointment. Addiction and a desire to escape the physical world are common. You can attract people who are unhealthy, addicted, and abusive because of idealizing others. Sacrificing sexual urges and having platonic relationships where sex is not a concern is common. Spiritual sex that transforms the physical is something you strive for. Make sure you find the right relationship partner who is dependable and can give the same energy you give to them. Try to pick your sexual partners carefully and be cautious about sharing your body with others that you do not know well, because you are a person who experiences a spiritual, energetic connection and can find it hard to break up.

There could be suffering involving other people's resources, inheritances, and property. Feeling deceived or lied to regarding material possessions can cause confusion. You might feel like you are fooled easily because you are overly trusting. Misunderstandings occur due to miscommunication and high expectations. There is a tendency for Neptune here to only see the good in people or believe what it wants to believe. Learning to see things from a spiritual perspective and practically is your greatest test.

Pluto in the Eighth

When Pluto is placed in the eighth house, powerful intuition and psychic abilities start in childhood. A natural born healer, your energy is soothing and intense. Healing energy fields such as Reiki, Pranic healing, healing touch, and even massage therapy will interest you. Others are drawn to your intense energy because you impact the environment with magnetism. Like moths to a flame people are attracted to you even if they don't understand why. You may not have understood why people wanted to be in your presence when you were younger. Sometimes people might have seemed afraid of you, either loving you or disliking you instantly. As you get older, your awareness shifts while you recognize the powerful energy you possess and try to use it to help others.

Making inner changes makes your personality powerful. Born with a highly sexual nature there is a strong desire for passion. Extremes rule your love life and affect intimate relationships. You will either have a lot of sexual activity in your life or none at all. Your sexual experiences run hot and cold. Feeling a deep connection to someone is critical for you to be physically intimate. Trusting others is a barrier to intimacy. As a natural psychologist who understands human behavior, you can see the motives of others clearly. You are often able to help people with their problems easily because you are perceptive. Bringing out people's secrets is your forte. People will feel vulnerable around you and feel as if everything they have repressed is called out of hiding. You make others face all the darker, hidden things in their personality. You bring out other people's secrets.

You are fascinated with death and the afterlife. It is important for you to understand what happens to the body after death and the process of soul evolution. Studying near death experiences, metaphysics, occultism, astrology, and any field that helps you better understand the purpose of life is beneficial. From a young age, you had an innate awareness of your own mortality. Fears of death or obsessions with morbid things can occur with this placement. This is a normal process and part of your personality but can also be an emotional wound. Your wound is the knowledge you have regarding the fragility of life. As you get older healing this wound can happen by becoming more spiritual. Your own understanding about the laws of the universe will help you overcome challenges and you will be known as a transformative healer.

Chiron in the Eighth

In astrology, Chiron is considered an asteroid and not a planet. Many astrologers believe that by looking at where Chiron is placed in the birth chart they can point to where a person needs to heal. It is also where you have the greatest capacity to heal others.

I want to discuss the energy of having Chiron in the eighth astrological house. I have been on my own journey trying to understand Chiron and was questioning if it actually had an impact on my life. It took me awhile to understand how Chiron influences us, but now I realize it has a transforming effect. When I first started studying astrology, I did not pay much attention to this asteroid. I started researching Chiron later in my life and I'm going to share my personal experience with having Chiron in the eighth. I have this placement and its conjunct my Moon and Jupiter.

For the past 12 years I have experienced many transforming and painful experiences. I have heard similar stories and intense experiences from clients. The first thing I noticed was many people describe Chiron as the wounded healer. I wanted to figure out for myself what the difference was between Chiron and Pluto. The planet Pluto shows where we have a wound and where we have potential to heal our wounds. The Chiron wound seems to remain and always be there under the surface. Wounds stay with us as a reminder of what we have been through. An imprint on our soul, similar to a tattoo that is always seen or a scar that remains.

There is often a cycle of being wounded by the people we love and trust. Being wounded can manifest in many ways verbally, emotionally, sexually, physically, and energetically. The wounding typically happens when we are involved in intimate relationships. It can start out at a young age such as being bullied or picked on as a child. When we look at the eighth house, we understand that it's the house of death, sex, transformation, rebirth, intimacy, sacrifice, other people's resources, and the house of intense things. These intense things can be painful reminders of how cruel people can be.

Death, loss, grief, sadness, loneliness are the wounds of Chiron. These wounds tend to develop through intimate relationships with people who are in our inner circle and with those who we have chosen to trust and have relationships with. Each wound makes you stronger, braver, and more courageous. When Chiron is in the eighth house, you always feel that people want to hurt you. You are more empathic and sensitive than most people. How people treat you can leave marks on your soul. The actions of others often shock you and cause you to retreat within.

I truly believe that Chiron in the eighth house brings a special energy. Many people with this placement have told me they feel like other people use them, manipulate, and hurt them. Chiron in the eighth house people want loyalty from others but they feel people are never loyal to them. Feeling like other people always take your kindness for granted creates a need to withdraw and protect yourself. Through the process of being wounded, people with Chiron in the eighth house develop a very passionate desire to help others. Understanding other people's losses and heartache comes naturally. Their wounds are right on the surface and always with them, like a scar that never fully heals. Scars show toughness and power.

People with unhealed pain are drawn to eighth house Chiron people. Many people seek healing from you and this can become a lonely placement. You feel like no one can help you heal and you have to do it on your own. Wounds come through feeling abandoned, tossed out, and betrayed. You might feel guilty and believe that you deserve being hurt. Shame can cloud your vision making it difficult to move forward.

Opening up and sharing deep parts of yourself with others is when Chiron transforms you. Being vulnerable and trusting others is a karmic lesson. You found your soul mate or at least you thought you did. You made a mistake and trusted someone, that is not your fault. I think the hardest thing about this placement is feeling that we can't trust others. Scars are a constant reminder of what you have been through. Like the phoenix bird rising from the ashes, the eighth house Chiron person rises, transforms and burns off the past in order to move forward.

Abandonment is often associated with Chiron. He was abandoned by his parents and then hurt by Hercules; he retreated into his cave to try to heal his wounds by himself. No matter what he does, the wounds are still there, serving as a reminder of what he went through. These wounds remain a part of him, his scars a reminder of his true purpose. His true purpose is to become a wounded healer. Chiron becomes known as a teacher for many people. This is the same destiny for people with Chiron in the eighth house. They are destined to become "wounded healers".

Eighth house Chiron people find their way through feeling needed and experiencing deep connections with others. They have a very calming effect upon other people. People say their energy is very healing and that is one reason people are drawn to them. As they begin to draw people into their lives, this helps them heal the deep trust and vulnerability issues they have been struggling with. They begin to learn to love themselves and trust their own intuition again. They stop before they sacrifice themselves for others. They learn not to sacrifice their happiness and be a martyr, even when they attract all these people that have a lot of problems that just take from them. Chiron in the eighth people develop a sense of aloneness and this can be a strength which leads to independence. They realize they don't need anyone to fulfill them, and that their own happiness and healing and understanding and growth come from within. That is your superpower.

The true power of Chiron is that special healing energy that lives within a person. It emanates out into the environment and draws people into your web. When Chiron is in the eighth house there is constant inner healing being experienced at all times. You know that you are constantly being reborn. The old self is stripped away and the old personality is transformed. Emotions change and it feels like you have died and changed overnight. Chiron in the eighth house people feel reborn daily, like a snake shedding its old skin morphing into a whole new version of yourself. Eventually this cycle will repeat itself.

When wounds are ignited, you will realize that you are meant to heal. Don't be afraid of having this placement. You can find happiness and healing. Having Chiron in the eighth house is actually an amazing placement because it heals you from the inside out. The true lesson is learning to depend on yourself and find a deep bond within.

North Node in the Eighth House (Scorpio)

The North Node represents your soul mission this lifetime. The personality traits of the astrological sign that the North Node is in are the traits that your soul needs to develop this lifetime. It's new territory and can be very uncomfortable. It is not easy to embrace this new energy because it's painful. From my experience, this is the most painful placement of the North Node. North Node in Scorpio is known to be the most difficult because it forces change. I want to focus on some tips and strategies to help you embrace the positive aspects of this placement.

You will feel the pull towards your North Node energy during your first Saturn Return which starts around age 27. For the first time in your life, you will start to feel things in your chart and become aware of feelings similar to the eighth house and Scorpio. Releasing energy patterns, relationships, mental blocks, and karma of the South Node will take time. North Node in Scorpio people have to let go of Taurus personality traits. The South Node represents your deeper soul, personality, and what you've already mastered in past lives. In this lifetime destroying those personality traits that no longer serve is the mission. These traits need to be released, changed, buried, and transformed.

Taurus energy rules the second house and involves learning lessons about security and comfort. As a previous Taurus, you will crave security, financial stability, and comfort in life. Taureans love material security, owning nice things, having a roof over their head, eating good food, beautiful art surrounding them, and money in the bank for a rainy day. Security will be tested and you will be forced out of your comfort zone. This can be a painful process because Scorpio is all about death which represents transformative change.

The person with this node is in a constant pull between death and rebirth throughout their entire life. These nodes are really powerful. Learning eighth house energy is extremely important, and you really have to understand your inner Taurus nature and accept that you cannot be a Taurus anymore. You need to start looking at how you can embrace the personality traits of the sign Scorpio. Focus on embracing this new energy that's foreign to you, maybe uncomfortable, and difficult at times. It's not warm and fuzzy feelings like the Taurus South Node. It's a little bit scary and a little bit painful to become a Scorpio but it forces you to grow.

Start consciously doing things to move towards your North Node personality traits. Read everything you can about Scorpio. Letting go of all the negative traits of Taurus and embracing the positive traits of Scorpio is the lesson. Scorpios are resilient, hide emotions, cut people off easily, and use their powerful personality to achieve goals. Ending things and moving forward releasing the past comes naturally for Scorpios. They're like, "Okay, I'm done with this. I'm moving on," and they will push forward.

Taureans struggle with doing that because they are connected to the past. People with Taurus South Node enjoy reminiscing about their childhood, roots, family, and previous experiences. Connections to childhood friends, lovers, and memories make it hard to let go. Change can be difficult and this node forces you to transform your entire personality. Shredding the comfortable parts of yourself and facing new uncomfortable aspects of your personality.

Focusing on the future is what Scorpio North Node people need to learn. Focusing on what's positive in your life and putting effort into manifesting new goals, and new memories is critical. Psychological endings are needed to get in touch with your soul mission. Letting go of things that hold you back or keep you stuck in the past is the true power of the Scorpio North Node. Being a healer, finding strength, embracing spirituality, and becoming a survivor is the mission of the North Node Scorpio person.

The only way to become strong is through experiencing pain. Unfortunately, emotional pain can be very intense. Feeling that you have to sacrifice something for others is associated with these nodes. Releasing things is more difficult for people with the South Node in Taurus. They are known to stay in learning patterns for way too long. Scorpio North Node people can stay in unhappy relationships and jobs due to fears of change. They don't like change. When they try to change it happens in baby steps. They will never make huge changes without planning. It takes time for them to learn how to do this, and it will not happen overnight.

You're destined to be healers, psychotherapists, and counselors who help people with emotional trauma. I have this node and I've experienced several lessons that are similar to what clients have shared with me. Many astrology books describe these nodes as the most challenging and painful. This node creates strength of character through difficult life experiences. By having things you care about stripped away from you, there is greater resilience. A strong, passionate nature develops with time and an inner wisdom.

Releasing South Node Taurus energy of needing comfort and constant stability will be the greatest challenge. It's okay to have comfort and stability in your life, but the problem is that Taurus South Node people tend to hold on to all these things too tightly. This can prevent growth as a person. Never struggling for survival, you will be blessed with material things. Part of the lesson of this node is learning to release attachments. By letting go of material things you can shake off outworn ideas, beliefs, and behaviors.

North Node Scorpio people experience many deaths and rebirths. Finding a way to live a simple, peaceful, and spiritual life is important. Many clients tell me that after the age of 60 which is after they survived their second Saturn Return, they have now released everything from their lives that made them feel stagnant and prevented growth. Developing deep soul mate bonds in this lifetime is their destiny.

Mastering everything Scorpio is important. Attracting Scorpio friends and coworkers will help you understand this new energy. Releasing material possessions and the need for financial security creates a shift. Learn to be more generous and less controlling. Find spiritual hobbies such as astrology, tarot, energy healing, crystal healing, yoga, and meditation. Find what you love to do and have that be your spiritual outlet. Forgiving others and starting a brand-new life creating new memories for the future is the ultimate goal.

Transits through the Eighth

Transit Sun in the Eighth House

When the Sun transits the eighth house, transformation and psychological change will be a focus in your life. Leaving things behind that are not satisfying and searching for something more fulfilling will be on the forefront of your mind. This transit makes you want to withdraw into your inner shell and reflect deeply on the life you have lived so far. You might feel more emotional, depressed, lonely, and frustrated during this transit. Extreme emotions will flow during this time and you might feel more secretive. Partnerships might be tested which brings up uncomfortable feelings, fears, and anxieties. Issues from the past and old emotional wounds can be stirred up to heal once and for all. Anything that was not dealt with will have to be felt at this time. Your personality will undergo extensive changes that can be painful. Talking to a counselor during this time might be helpful.

Transit Moon in the Eighth House

When the Moon transits the eighth house, you will feel a heavier energy during this time. Intense and powerful emotions will hit you out of the blue. Be cautious getting caught up in unpleasant emotions. This is a fast transit and does not last long. You might regret what you said to others once the Moon transitions into the ninth house. Feeling more sensitive, vulnerable, and irritated is common. You may cry easily and have a hard time concealing feelings during this time. If you're typically not a jealous person you will feel more distrusting of intimate partners during this transit. If there are things you have repressed this transit will awaken them. The past comes back to haunt you and feelings have to be acknowledged.

Transit Mercury in the Eighth House

When Mercury transits the eighth house, thoughts are jumbled and overshadowed by anxiety. Communication can seem intense, deep, and conflicted. There can be difficulties thinking things through logically. Anything you try to communicate or share during this time will be based on inner feelings and this causes relationship issues. Intense thoughts cloud your mind making it difficult not to dig deep below the surface of what people say. Tension and conflict are heightened. If you're typically social, you'll want to avoid superficial conversations during this transit craving something more real and serious. Your thoughts are transformed during this time bringing greater awareness.

Transit Venus in the Eighth House

Venus transiting the eighth house intensifies emotions and desires for sexual intimacy. Your true needs and vulnerable areas will be exposed during this time. There may be insecure feelings and an increased need to focus on intimate relationships or a love interest. Being attracted to intense, mysterious people is common during this transit. Increased sexual desires and a need for developing deep, lasting partnerships can happen with this transit. Be cautious about unpleasant emotions such as jealousy, revenge, anger, hate, and possessiveness. These feelings will need to be balanced to avoid conflict with others. You need relationships that touch your body and soul. This transit helps you get in touch with your needs and desires.

Transit Mars in the Eighth House

Mars transiting the eighth will bring powerful, passionate emotional and sexual needs. Feeling angry and resentful about a lack of sex is common. Feeling like you don't have control can cause anxiety. Power struggles occur in relationships and an increased need to express feelings of anger, aggression, and passion will happen. This time is full of conflict and you might feel like you are walking on eggshells. Tension is in the air. Transformation comes by addressing deep seated issues that need to be expressed. You feel intense and on edge but perceive things much easier right now. You spot fake people right away and may cut ties. Superficial situations will rouse irritability and a desire to lash out. Disputes with spouse, family, or a significant other is common, and if there is a business partner there can be disagreements.

Transit Jupiter in the Eighth House

Jupiter transiting the eighth house is a positive transit but there can be challenges. This transit helps you open up emotionally and feel more generous with others. Encouraging and motivating others helps you achieve your goals. Good luck comes through relationship partners who teach you about yourself. Jupiter brings a positive, uplifting energy to the heavy eighth house energies. You may feel more comfortable digging down deep into your power and control issues. Healing the past often comes easily with this transit and it's like you are finally ready to move forward thanks to Jupiter. This is a time of growth and things might be stripped away to create room for better things. Financial blessings and even benefits through inheritance are common during this time.

Transit Saturn in the Eighth House

Saturn transiting through the eighth house can be painful. During this time, you will be tested beyond measure and feel heavy demands. Emotional choices from earlier in life will need to be reevaluated. Karmic relationships and balancing your actions towards others are common during this time. Someone from the past will reappear to challenge your livelihood, relationships, and goals. Intimate relationships are tested and you may have to let go of something or someone you love the most. Sometimes you choose material security over passion, deep love, and intimacy. Choosing material security over true love might be something you regret when you grow older. Personality traits and patterns that are negative will need to be transformed and forever changed. Power struggles are common and if there are any hidden addictions in your life, you'll be forced to face them head-on. Secrets will be revealed and you could feel very uncomfortable during this transit. Undergoing change and dealing with issues related to sexuality, shared finances and resources will affect many areas of your life. This will be a serious time where you feel heavy burdens and struggle to find happiness. Karmic debts have to be repaid. Growth comes through pain, sacrifice, and rebirth.

Transit Uranus in the Eighth House

When Uranus transits the eighth house there will be unexpected changes, shocking events, and loss. Death of a loved or someone close to you can be blindsiding, causing you to struggle to comprehend emotions that come up. Death can also be symbolic and involve changes that impact your identity. If you are living a stagnant life, this transit will shake you up and spit you out. It might take time to figure out what is happening to your life. The best way to overcome this transit is to accept this new energy. Learn to embrace these triggers and feel free to explore new emotions, thoughts, beliefs, and personality traits that you did not know existed within. Attachments will be stripped away, especially those that are not helping you grow. Bottom line, you have to release things and let go of old ways of doing things. Uranus triggers repressed feelings to come up and you will face darker parts of yourself that you never knew existed. You might find yourself involved in taboo behavior or expressing things you normally would never express. You want to rebel from boring, routine, and practical life responsibilities. Exciting people can enter your life and wake you up. Just be careful about changing your life during this time because this energy is not stable and can change instantly. This transit causes tremendous emotional pain that can affect your physical health if not handled appropriately. This house rules sex and sometimes you will become more open about exploring and experimenting with new ways of showing love with your partner. Be careful about getting involved in secret affairs or hidden love relationships because any relationship developed during this transit can end abruptly, tragically, and unexpectedly. Once this transit is over you will look back and realize that you are a completely different person than you were before.

Transit Neptune in the Eighth House

When Neptune transits the eighth house, there are struggles with boundaries. Addressing tendencies of being idealistic and seeing things with rose-colored glasses can help balance emotions. There is a heightened sensitivity, increased psychic experiences, deep dreams, and a desire to bond on a deeper level with a significant other. Soul mate relationships and sexual bonds can cause suffering, especially if you are sacrificing your own needs for someone who does not appreciate you. Be cautious about giving too much of yourself to others and never getting anything in return. Developing stronger boundaries during this transit will help protect you from being taken advantage of emotionally, materially, and financially. Learn to say no and put yourself first. Be extra careful about idealism and only seeing the good in others. Be more realistic and practical with your emotions during this time. Stop giving all your love, energy, and attention to others. This might be a good time to seek counseling and work on deep healing.

Transit Pluto in the Eighth House

When Pluto transits the eighth house there is an intense, emotional, life changing experience. Death of loved ones is common during this transit. There will be a time when you have to grieve, organize a funeral, and handle the material resources of a deceased loved one. Inheritances are common during this transit and they can be financial or emotional benefits. Repressed emotions and unhealed issues relating to sexuality and death will be exposed. It will feel like Pandora's box is being opened and all those deep, dark secrets, and parts of yourself are under attack. Facing the shadow part of your personality during this transit will make you feel vulnerable. Intense love affairs can be experienced or it's possible to get involved with individuals who mirror the darker side of your personality. Fascination, obsession, and jealousy can be intensified causing dramatic conflicts and relationship problems. During this transit you may feel victimized or be the one victimizing others in some way. Power and control issues will be brought to the surface. Divorce and ending love relationships is common when Pluto moves into the eighth. Healing unpleasant memories, emotions, and addictive behaviors will help you transform. Be cautious about money schemes but focus on joint finances and fix any issues with money that exist in your life. Power and issues with exerting power in your life will be tested.

Chapter Fourteen

Eighth House Phoenixes' Greatest Strengths and Weaknesses

The eighth house is where you are tested. It is where you will come face to face with your shadow self and parts of yourself that are hidden from other people. There are often personality traits and things about yourself that lay dormant within that you are not even aware of.

I realized my own planets in the eighth house showed me where my greatest weaknesses and strengths were. I finally recognized the connection between the planet placements in the eighth as well as the eighth house transits that I had lived through.

Figuring out what your greatest weakness is comes easily when you look at the planets in your eighth house. If you don't have planets in the eighth house, you will want to look at the sign on the cusp of the eighth. For instance, if Taurus is on the eighth house cusp you will have difficulties letting go, forgiving others, and you can be possessive of those you care about. Your greatest weakness could be a special person, emotion, behavior, or the past. It can manifest in how you deal with emotions, show love, family troubles, work issues, unhealed trauma, grief, or emotional pain. These types of intense situations are part of eighth house weaknesses. You might not realize what your greatest weakness is but you can start looking at the specific planets in the eighth house and what aspects are occurring. You can gain deeper self-awareness by paying more attention to the energies.

Below are planets in the eighth, specific weaknesses that might be experienced, and positive ways to overcome these energies.

Eighth House Sun
When the Sun is in the eighth house your greatest weakness can be something associated with your identity. It can also involve something that has to do with your father or the father's side of the family. There might be loss of the father figure at a young age. Inheriting something from your father or from his family such as personality traits, secretiveness, addictions, anger, or psychic abilities is common.

Eighth House Moon
When the Moon is in the eighth the emotional nature and emotional vulnerability can be the greatest weakness. Emotional highs and lows are common as well as experiencing periods of depression. The Moon represents the mother figure and sometimes there are difficulties concerning mothering or lack of nurturing. You might be very attached to your mother but there are often emotional issues involving heartbreak and trust. There might be loss of the mother figure at a young age or separation. There can be painful transformative experiences with the Moon here and this makes you a very sensitive person with empathic abilities. Your greatest weakness could be controlling your emotions and learning to protect yourself from being taken advantage of by others.

Eighth House Venus
When Venus is in the eighth house your greatest weakness usually involves how you express and show love. It also affects the type of people that you're attracted to. Venus in the eighth is a very deep placement that craves intimacy and deep bonding with another person. Seeking intense relationships based on passion can lead to heartache, jealousy, possessiveness, and control issues. You might also struggle with self-esteem and appearance. Instead of seeking peace you might prefer challenging relationships.

Eighth House Mercury

Mercury represents your mind, thoughts and beliefs. In the eighth house it can manifest as obsessive thoughts that create anxiety, worry and negativity. This placement can make you a serious thinker who struggles with expressing yourself. You might find it difficult to talk about feelings because finding the right words, and trusting other people can be challenging. You might have a wound involving sharing personal information and feeling betrayed by others who repeated it. This weakness can make you withdraw, create secretiveness, and cause you to hide your beliefs from others.

Eighth House Mars

When Mars is in the eighth it creates a very powerful drive and passion. Sometimes there are struggles with intimacy. Suppressing strong urges is common and experiences of energy explosions that are impulsive. Mars here also involves the types of people you feel sexually attracted to. Attracting controlling, powerful, and dominant personalities is common. A desire to have passion can cause relationship difficulties. Selfishness and passion to pursue deep desires can become addictive.

Eighth House Jupiter

Jupiter in the eighth from my experience is a positive placement. It protects you from the darker and more complicated eighth house energy. There is also another side to Jupiter besides bringing positivity, good luck, blessings, and inheritance. It can make you extremely giving, optimistic and kind. Sometimes people will take you for granted or take advantage of your kindness. It can be hard for you to turn people away who need help. You enjoy helping others which can become a weakness if not balanced. You become drained easily because you are extremely generous of your time and energy. Be cautious about loaning people money and sacrificing your own needs for others.

Jupiter is very protective and can cause you to be too trusting of others. Developing stronger boundaries and learning more about yourself will help protect your precious energy.

Eighth House Saturn
Saturn in the eighth can create a restrictive energy causing fears of bonding with others. You might repress your true nature and restrict expressions of love and communication. This placement makes you feel overly serious and rigid. Holding strict routines, expectations for yourself and others can be challenging. A strong sense of duty can turn into a burden. Saturn here is focused on practical matters, material success, and security but it especially heightens a need to be in control. Trying to control people or the outcome of situations is your greatest weakness. Your greatest strength can be a strong determination to achieve goals. Feeling responsible and wanting to do the right thing can cause distress.

Eighth House Neptune
Neptune in the eighth house makes you psychic and open to energy in your surroundings. You are like a light that attracts people that need healing to you. There could be escapist tendencies and a desire to numb yourself from heavy eighth house energy through alcohol, drugs, relationships, and sex. A sensitivity to other people's problems, lack of boundaries, and a desire to escape from painful emotions are common with this placement. Your greatest weakness is absorbing other people's emotions such as depression, anxiety, and sadness. Idealism can blind you making it difficult to see situations clearly. Romanticism and falling in love with unhealthy people can cause difficulties. Putting others' needs before your own and continuing unhealthy relationships can cause suffering.

Eighth House Uranus
When Uranus is in the eighth house, there is an unexpected energy

that shakes up your life and causes intense changes. Experiencing many ups and downs of emotions and being blindsided is a common experience. Most people like comfort and stability. Feeling out of control when your life is turned upside down can happen with Uranus here. Experiencing unhealed wounds and feeling things that you believed had already been healed is common. Your greatest weakness could be that you get too comfortable with unexpected changes and avoid routine. When life gets too comfortable, you may believe that you need to shake things up. This creates forced change that might be detrimental to your happiness. Enjoy periods of stability in your life.

Eighth House Pluto

Pluto in the eighth house makes you perceptive and psychic with a desire to hide things from others. You can see through other people and are a very deep person. Serious and cautious about showing vulnerability, you tend to repress emotions. You can see other people's weaknesses well, but your own weaknesses are often hidden from you. Other people can trigger your weaknesses and bring them out to the surface. Pluto wants to have total power and control over its emotions. Your greatest weakness would be difficulty trusting others and preferring to be alone and doing things your own way. There is always a fear of being totally vulnerable and dependent on anyone.

Eighth House Chiron

Chiron is the wounded healer and when it is placed in the eighth house you will experience wounds through intimacy and love relationships. When Chiron is in the eighth house your greatest weakness is often giving your trust to people who don't deserve it. The lesson of this placement is healing your wounds in order to help others heal. Giving too much is a weakness. Feeling others' pain and wanting to relieve it can become a vicious cycle that is difficult to break. Avoid taking on other people's karma and learn to detach from the pain of others.

Identifying your greatest weakness is important and it can help you understand your greatest strength. Embracing the shadow side of your personality is a spiritual lesson of the eighth house.

Eighth House Phoenixes' Insights

"As an eighth house Sun, Mercury and Mars my strengths would be having psychic intuition, clairvoyance, and seeing the beauty in darkness. My weaknesses include having had obsessiveness to the point of self-harm, pushing extremely when not needed, and having an overall sense of melancholia even when everything is fine."
– A.S.

"I have the Sun, Venus, Saturn, Mars, Mercury all in the eighth house. My greatest strength is I am very intuitive and can read people very well. I get good and bad vibes and am also a very good listener. A lot of people come to me for advice or just for someone to talk to. I am a very calm person and have learned to control my anger. My greatest weakness is I am introverted and very quiet. I struggle with speaking up around people I am not comfortable with."
– C.M.

"I have Sun, Mercury, Venus, Neptune and Mars in the eighth. My strength is facing really bad things head-on and without hesitation. Instant survivor mode kicks in, by looking at things from the outside and going into problem solving mode immediately lessens the drama. My weakness is not being able to contain myself when someone lies to me or shows me they are fake. I am getting better and instead of calling them out, I use the energy to close them off from my life by avoiding them altogether. Trust is a huge issue for me. There are some good actors and actresses out there!"
– M.S.

"My greatest strength is my resilience and ability to transform and not get sucked under with the undertow of life. My greatest challenge is enmeshment and bonding. It is knowing when enough is really enough and choosing myself. As Remy said: boundaries."
– B.L.

"My strength is I am highly intuitive and pick up on subtleties in my environment. My weakness is I can be very harsh with my words."
– D.D.

"My strength is resilience and resourcefulness. My weakness is that from time to time I spiral down into very dark places which can be hard to get out of."
– A.I.

"With Mars, Venus, Jupiter, Cancer and Mercury in the eighth house, my greatest strength is deep perception with a tenacity to uncover root causes and to cognize solutions. My greatest weakness is existential depression with a nagging ever present melancholy."
– M.R.

"I have the Sun, Moon, and Chiron in the eighth house. I am finally accepting that I will experience a lot of traumas and losses in life which I have come to realize have helped me transform into a stronger person as I grow older. I just turned 30 and recently lost my dad. My greatest strength is probably that I still choose to live and love despite all the losses I have experienced. My weakness is that sometimes my emotions get the best of me. I tend to easily absorb energy around me."
– T.F.

"My strength is resilience, tenacity and determination. I pick up things that are not said and often see more than is said. My weakness is it takes me a long time to detach my emotions and involvement from

a situation or person."
– S.L.

"Bouncing back from everything stronger and better is my strength. My weakness is caring for the wrong people."
– S.F.

"Seeing through everyone I meet is my strength and jealousy is my weakness."
– C.J.

"I have Sun, Moon, Mercury, Venus and Chiron in the eighth house. My strength is my intuition, ability to see the beauty in anything, acceptance of the light and dark aspects of myself and in others. My weakness is caring too much, having extremely strong convictions, seeking comfort in cemeteries, forests and with those who have passed on."
– B.K.

"My greatest strength is perseverance and my greatest weakness is self-sabotage."
– M.S.

"My greatest strength is that I rise like a phoenix from painful love situations. My greatest weakness is I need some drama and intensity or I am not interested. I have both Venus and Mars in my eighth house."
– A.G.

"As an eighth house Sun, Venus, Mercury and Chiron person I would say my greatest strength is being able to understand people on a deep level. My greatest weakness is not knowing how to help myself the way I help others."
– K.W.

"My strength is resilience and resourcefulness. My weakness is from time to time I spiral down into very dark places which [are] very hard to get out of."
– A.I.

"My greatest strength is that I am highly intuitive and pick up on subtleties. Being very harsh with my words is my weakness."
– D.D.

"My greatest strength is to keep going no matter what. My greatest weakness is rage. I have Sun, Uranus, Venus and Jupiter in the eighth."
– B.B.

"Listening and loyalty are my strengths. Never feeling truly loved is my weakness. Sun, Mercury, Mars and North Node are all in eighth house."
– A.O.

"Not wanting to show vulnerability is my greatest weakness."
– S.H.

"My Sun and Mercury are in the eighth. My greatest strengths are my intuitive and research abilities, and honesty. I have several weaknesses including mental illness such as depression, post-traumatic stress disorder, and feelings of jealousy." – M.R.

Chapter Fifteen

Eighth House Phoenixes' Personal Wisdom

North Node in the Eighth from M.A., U.S.A.

"Spirituality has always been a big part of my life since I was a child. I got interested in the occult, spirituality, metaphysics, and astrology when I was 15 years old. I had a near death experience as a child and I can still remember it. I have always had the deep desire to merge with a man and have such a deep connection with him so that through intimacy I can transcend in a way and expand my consciousness. I have been pursuing this since I was 19 years old. At first, this desire was not conscious. As the years go by, this soul desire of mine to completely merge and experience something divine through intimacy is getting stronger and stronger.

I am still learning to be gentler with myself and to focus on self-care. This has never been easy for me, especially when I was younger. I am also trying to change my emotional patterns and not be emotionally dependent on external things.

I easily feel others' feelings and wounds, sometimes to the point that they become my own but it is not always like that. Sometimes I succeed in setting some boundaries, other times I struggle. I have energy healing abilities and help people when I can. I like to help people find a sense of spirituality in their lives and help them understand why something happens to them, and how they can learn from experiences. I kind of feel it is my purpose to do these things."

Mars in the Eighth from A.G., Sweden

"I have Mars retrograde in the eighth house. To summarize what I have been experiencing and what I've been through, I can definitely compare my life experience to a sequence of catastrophic events. It felt as if I was born to die many times in order for me to time after time be born again, though in a totally different skin. Metamorphosis, cataclysm, change, and digging deep are the keys of what I have been experiencing. My Mars is retrograde so that my Martian energy, which at the beginning manifested itself in Leo, was very destructive, yet rather self-destructive. I would turn inwards, against myself and experienced several suicide attempts.

Self-loathing, rage explosion, impulsiveness, self-destructiveness, stormy relationships, and erratic behavior have hallmarked the first part of my life until I turned 28. I was a ticking bomb, always angry and on the verge of the implosion. I've always felt overwhelmed by an upheaval of emotions. They are always very intense, sometimes it feels as if I don't have any skin protecting me against feeling too much. When I turned 29, I became more rational and much less reckless.

The main feature this placement has gifted me with is the ability to see through people and to dig down six feet under getting to the root cause of things. My intuition is highly developed and when it comes to researching or carrying out detective-like tasks I can really deliver. Mars in eighth moving towards Libra is making me increasingly diplomatic, tactful and even wiser. Reading people and seeing through the mask is a gift I now couldn't live without. This personality trait literally saved my skin on several occasions.

Other than this plutonian capacity of transformation, metamorphosis, and regeneration, when I needed it, I am also able to cut people and negative things out completely. To sum it up, at the beginning this volatile and violent energy was a destructive force. I've now learned to catalyze it, using it in a much more constructive way. It has become a creating, shaping force rather than a curse but I really had to go through hell to learn how to handle it.

I may not be inheriting anything from my father. I am estranged from my entire family, because of different kinds of abuse I have systematically been put through since I was a child. So even here there's been a sharp cut with no turning back, it has been catastrophic and painful but utterly necessary. It felt like death but eventually I was born again and it marked my rebirth.

I have developed a very strong interest in the occult and I am very attracted to darkness, witchcraft, cemeteries, fairies, and all mysteries of death and the underworld. When it comes to the sexual drive, it has always been very strong."

Saturn, Uranus and Neptune in the Eighth from K.T., U.S.A.

"I had a lot of strange things happen throughout my life, odd situations, and freak accidents. I go through periods of obsessing over knowledge and the meaning of life, the universe, and religions. I have lost a lot of people in my life and had many ailments with my health."

Mercury in the Eighth from E.D., U.S.A.

"I have a hard time forgiving people, and being open to people is something I am working on."

Moon, North Node in the Eighth from K.G., United Kingdom

"I lost my beloved mum at the tender age of eleven. It took me years to come to terms with my loss. I recently found out that this is a common experience for people with the Moon in the eighth house."

Sun and Saturn in the Eighth from T.B., U.S.A.

"I believe these placements make it hard having boundaries in relationships and most of my relationships are tumultuous and ever changing."

Moon in the Eighth from S.J., London, England

"The Moon deals with the mother so this is where I will start. My mother was very young when she gave birth to me. She was sixteen. Although young, my parents married and then divorced when I was three years old. The chaos of my parents arguing meant that I was eager to learn to speak as a young child as a form of protection and also so I could ask questions, therefore I learned to speak very early.

I always felt my mum was detached from me and she was more interested in friends and partying than looking after me. After the divorce, I lived with my mum and her friend Kate. I felt closer to my mum's friend Kate and wished she was my mum instead. But their friendship ended when my mum started a new relationship with my stepdad when I was five. Growing up I always wanted to have long beautiful hair like other little girls did. My mum took me to the hairdressers and had my shoulder length hair cut off short like a boy. I was always feminine and my mum did everything to make me look like a boy. I wanted dresses, she dressed me in boys' clothes. I don't know why my femininity made her feel so spiteful towards me. My mum never wanted me around and instead I found myself begging her friends to read to me or to talk to me as I always felt completely ignored. She didn't even want to make proper food. I remember I was always fed tinned macaroni or sandwiches.

As previously stated, my mum started a new relationship when I was five. My mum didn't leave him until I was 20 and she had my younger brother with him a few years later when I was nine. My new stepdad was not easy to deal with. He was very controlling from the start. He controlled my mum and me and what hurt the most was when he was being abusive to me, because my mum would ignore it, and put her head down. My mum would mostly ignore his behavior but she did have violent outbursts now and then as his behavior got too much for her. I remember on one occasion she chased him down the road with a knife. This was due to an argument that occurred because my mum had issues with alcohol and drugs. This was done in front of me. I saw my mum with the knife and my stepdad run out of the house and my mum chase him.

When I was 10 my mum had bad epilepsy which was brought on by drugs and alcohol. I was at primary school and it was lunch time. My teacher came and found me and said my mum had called the school to ask them to send me home to look after her and my one-year-old brother as she had an epileptic seizure. I got home and within 30 minutes she was on the floor having a seizure. I had to look after not only her but my baby brother. I had to keep this a secret from my stepdad. He was at work throughout the day so he didn't know what was going on. I had to act normal when he got home. I had to keep it a secret because if he found out my mum had a seizure it would cause an argument because her seizures were related to drugs and alcohol.

As I got older my mum would tell me inappropriate things about her personal life. She once told me when I was around 12 years old about how she had an affair with her boss when she was working part-time in a care home. I had to keep her secrets. I wasn't allowed to say anything. I became very spiritual around the age of nineteen. I had nothing except my spiritual beliefs. I asked the universe while I was living in a hostel for a flat and wrote down in detail what I wanted. It's like the universe heard me because I got exactly what I asked for.

I developed my spirituality and became interested in psychics, mediums, and tarot cards as well as astrology. I now make money doing readings for people. As part of my spiritual beliefs, I learned that self-healing is crucial to a person's personal growth. I did shadow work which is still ongoing. I found out that I have a hard time expressing my emotions and tend to bottle them up. The lesson I needed to learn was that my emotions are just as important as others'. I went through a phase in life from 22 up until recently, age 32, trying to reconnect with myself emotionally. I was very sensitive emotionally as a child and I felt like that part of myself died and I became desperate to revive it. I went through therapy to help.

My anxiety became so bad I had terrible panic attacks. This made me feel weak and vulnerable and, to be honest, useless as I couldn't even leave the house without experiencing really bad physical anxiety symptoms. I was desperate to overcome my anxiety and deal with the intense strong emotions that were starting to come back to me. I had to become my own therapist. I wrote about my feelings in poems which helped me release the bottled-up emotions. When I was on my own, I would listen to music which expressed my feelings.

I also realized that my own inner dialogue needed work. I was my own worst enemy. Constantly being hard on myself, I had to work on that. I also had to learn how to sit with my anxiety and pain. I had been so numb inside for so long I forgot how to do that. I had to learn to reprocess my emotions and not repress them. I learned to speak about my pain and even writing this is very healing for me."

Saturn, Venus, and North Node in the Eighth from L.A., U.S.A.

"My North Node in the eighth has offered lessons on intimacy, entanglement, loyalty, other people's resources, and the process of psychological healing and wounding. I had to chart my own course as an Aries North Node while still being closely connected to a very tightknit codependent family. It's like untangling a knotted ball of thread, string by string. Therapy and astrology are a world of self-help, determination to keep going no matter what, a loyal partner, and perhaps divine grace has helped me on occasion.

It's hard to separate Saturn from Venus in my eighth, as they are so closely conjunct. Difficulty in relationships is a phrase that comes to mind, as well as a profound desire and simultaneous resistance to individuating. Feeling alienated and isolated, even among people, is also something I think can be seen in these placements but there is something very enduring about these placements too. I have been in a loyal marriage for over 25 years. The presence of Venus with Saturn seems to be a saving grace with difficulties and many lessons being hard, but there has always been something of value gleaned in the end.

On the subject of challenges, I think these placements lend a quality of being impacted by outside forces and the actions of others have often caused grief, stress, anger, and wounding. Many events have transpired in my life that were completely beyond my control. I have been well acquainted with death of family members, friends, boyfriends, and acquaintances.

My husband suffered a violent attack when we were in our mid-thirties and I attempted to fight off the attacker but not before he bit my husband's nose off. He went through many reconstructive surgeries as a result. In this same period of only about five months in 2003, he lost his good friend to a motorcycle accident and his 53-year-old mother to a short battle with cancer. Less than a month later, I became pregnant with our first child and had a very high-risk pregnancy, being hospitalized for six weeks prior to giving birth. He was born premature by scheduled C-section. The first year was challenging, but he is a healthy, brilliant 16-year-old now.

Lastly, in the last seven years I discovered I had two siblings that I was unaware of. I grew up with two sisters and I am the oldest. My father was an alcoholic but hid it very well and travelled extensively for work. It was devastating to find out he was not the person I believed him to be. Despite the infidelity, he stayed married to my mom who had her own battles with mental health. My parents went from rags to riches, and back again over the course of their marriage. To make a long story short, although we had our material needs taken care of as kids, my parents were emotionally unavailable. It was a situation where I often felt like the parent to my parents. In retrospect, I do believe my parents were narcissists but it's hard to separate that from the mental health and addiction issues.

As for the lessons learned from these placements. I'm approaching my 52nd birthday, so there have been many. To sum it up, I believe what doesn't kill you makes you stronger, it's cliché but true. Slow and steady wins the race. Resilience is everything. Patience is key. The older I get, the more adept I feel. I am at dealing with life's biggest challenges. For example, these placements prepared me to deal with the crazy show of 2020 with relative composure, and I feel like there isn't much I can't handle at this point. Not everyone has the courage, capacity, or even privilege of being able to go through many dark nights of the soul and come out the other side. People with these placements seem to be born with an innate ability to endure and rise above.

I often use the analogy of the phoenix rising from the ashes when I talk about these placements. I think the key is that the phoenix has to burn up before it can rise again."

Moon, Jupiter and Chiron in the Eighth
from C.T., U.S.A.

"I remember lying in bed at night thinking that I could die. I would lay there for hours worried. I would wonder what if something happened to me and what if I died. I would ask myself, 'Where will I go, will it hurt, what will happen to me?' I was afraid and always had to have a night light on and my door open. I was always afraid of the dark from a young age. I remember my mother telling me to go back to sleep, and that my dreams were not going to happen. She would tell me they were just dreams. I would wake up screaming a few nights every week and was a sleepwalker. According to my family, I would act out my dreams. One night I remember running down the hall and screaming, trying to get out of the door and my mother woke me up. I was acting out a dream. I would dream vividly, and at times, confused my dreams from real memories because that was how powerful they were. My mother told me I always woke her up in the night. I would play with imaginary friends and dance with them. I had a memory when I was older of dancing in my room as a child to the song the *Monster Mash* playing with my imaginary friends."

Moon in the Eighth House from A.E., Australia

"I have always felt the energy of situations before fully understanding them. Growing up, I was sort of a pawn used for the power plays between my mom and dad but didn't realize it until years later. I've learned to be selective with who I keep close and make sure that I trust the person before getting into a relationship. My Moon is in Aries and part of me feels like I'm destined to be alone, and a bigger part of me yearns to be able to trust someone with my whole being. Whenever I get too close too soon, I shut myself off and escape until I feel grounded again.

After all the deaths I've experienced throughout my life, this inspired me to live for myself. Each death brought me closer to my spirituality, but this taught me to fulfill my life and to work on my depression. I started getting interested in crystals and finding out their metaphysical properties and practicing meditation. I'm extremely guarded with my emotions and who I allow to know my true feelings and thoughts. I want to help others realize their strengths and fulfill their highest potential. I've realized that we are meant to undergo these changes and experiences in order to value the opposite to the fullest. Death puts into perspective how valuable life is. Sometimes we won't understand *why* we go through things at the time but the answers come later in life. Having my Moon in the eighth has taught me the gift of letting go and relying on myself when life gets tough. When I get lonely, I immerse myself in nature or go to the ocean and allow it to heal all that I'm unable to put into words. Something about the ocean just overcomes me with peace. I also have conversations with my parents now. Both are deceased and I've always felt like I could feel their messages to me from the other side."

Pluto in the Eighth from K.D., U.S.A.

"My third partner died of cancer. Looking back, he was the sweetest most loving man I ever met. His time on this earth was short enough to help me heal and learn. I often look back on it with fondness and regret. My true friends are limited since I learned early on the betrayal of so many, but the ones who are true and loyal resonate with my soul on deeper levels. Those closest to me, know my soul and come to me for answers and advice on life. They know my soul and heart to be as pure and my backbone as strong as all the hardships life has thrown at me.

I am currently learning astrology, something I have had an interest in since childhood.

I may not quite fully understand how all my placements have shaped my life but I hope to discover it one day. I can say I have experienced many ups and downs in my life, many traumas and hardships and many blessings. I can say that my servitude to the ones I love is strong and my path with God, although sometimes faltering, is something that keeps me here. Somehow, I understand my life holds greater meaning if not for me, then for those put in my life path."

Pluto in the Eighth from A.J., Serbia

"I was always hypersensitive and very emotional. I grew up in a cold environment where expressing emotions was not welcome or recognized. I felt distant with my mother who was suppressing her emotions and had depression and anxiety. My father is very strict and not connected to his emotions. I started going to psychotherapy and it took years to get to my emotions.

Maybe because my Moon in 12th squares Pluto in eighth house, which is in Scorpio. I had some kind of prenatal or birth trauma. I still go to psychotherapy and it helps me, but I noticed that the transit of Saturn through my twelfth house which is happening now makes me more emotional and brings a lot of pain, but still connects me with my emotions. I feel like I am a very emotional person, but that my emotions are always inside and it is hard for me to express them. Only in situations of loss and very difficult times can I reach them. Inside I always feel a lot."

Part Two

Mastering the Twelfth House

Your sacred space is where you can find yourself over and over again.
– Joseph Campbell

Chapter One

Solitude, Retreat, Isolation, and Seclusion

The twelfth house is associated with solitude. Spending time alone and being able to find time to retreat from the stresses of the world is extremely important for twelfth house people. I have always felt a desire to be alone, especially with my Sun in the twelfth house. Being by myself makes me feel better and brings peace. I could stay inside my home for days reading, listening to music, writing, and watching my favorite television shows. I needed to withdraw from social situations and isolate myself from the energy of others. I remember feeling exhausted after being at school and socializing with groups of people. I would look forward to getting home to my sanctuary. Being alone is my way of ensuring that I take care of my emotional and physical health. It is critical to my well-being and one of my self-care practices.

Twelfth house people need a place where they can retreat from the world. Some may find their home is the best place for them to isolate themselves and retreat. Others might find solace in nature or being outdoors near the mountains or water. Finding a healthy balance is the goal. Sometimes escaping from stressful situations can become excessive. Twelfth house people can become recluses and hermits, finding it difficult to go out into the world to live a practical life. There may be times they avoid people and social interaction. Many twelfth house people have shared with me their desire to have the house all to themselves and be able to sit in silence. It can be a blessing not to have another single living being around. People who do not have twelfth house planets will not understand these feelings. Most people find it difficult to be alone. I remember having friends who disliked ever being alone and always had to have someone to spend time with them.

When I was in college, I used to enjoy going out to eat by myself. I would take all my books and homework with me and study while I ate. The hostess staff would always act strange and I sensed they felt sorry for me. They would always ask if someone else would be joining me and I would always tell them the same thing each time. I would explain that I like being on my own and no one would be coming. There were times I would invite one or two friends, I always preferred small groups. I was extremely shy when younger and always an observer. At social gatherings I preferred staying away from others and watched them from a distance. My friends would always try to get me to go out with them when I was in college. I hated those situations and would try to force myself to go and be a supportive friend. Each and every time I would only be there about five minutes and then would ask for them to take me back to my dorm room or to my apartment. I learned quickly that I should always drive my own car in case I needed to escape and retreat back to where I felt most comfortable.

Twelfth house people cherish peace and harmony. They dislike anything that is negative and harsh. They will seek peace at all costs even if that means isolating themselves from things that cause stress. They must be cautious about developing unhealthy coping patterns and learn to balance the need to do things on their own. Avoiding reality and responsibilities is a negative coping pattern and can cause many issues in relationships.

Twelfth house people have a rich inner life full of imagination. They enjoy writing about how they feel and contemplating on the meaning of life. As natural psychologists they also like figuring out other people. They are empaths and this is why they have a strong need for seclusion. Twelfth house people absorb everything in the environment and take it on as their own. This ability can weigh them down and make it difficult to truly identify who they are and who others are. They are sensitive to energies and these things can become confusing if they don't have adequate time alone with their own thoughts.

Benefits come from meditation, mindfulness practices, and focusing within. Many enjoy meditation and find that yoga comes naturally for them. Focusing on breathing and stilling the mind helps enhance greater insights. Being alone helps relieve stress and anxiety. It is important for twelfth house people to have a sacred space in their home where they can be by themselves. If they have a spouse and children, it will be important for them to have this private place specifically to hibernate, withdraw, and seclude themselves. I have a special room in my house that I call my spiritual room. It is my space where I have all my favorite spiritual pictures, candles, books, and music. When I feel stressed, this is the special place I retreat to. I encourage twelfth house people to create a space that belongs only to them. Making time for solitude is important for anyone with twelfth house planets. They should not feel guilty about needing alone time because their soul needs it to function in the practical world.

Chapter Two

Psychic Abilities and Mystical Experiences

Twelfth house people are born with intuitive and empathic abilities. They have a vivid imagination and are extremely creative. When planets are placed in the twelfth house there are spiritual gifts similar to eighth house people. Twelfth house gifts tend to be more connected to the emotions and imagination. Watery, fluid and changeable the psychic experiences often come out of the blue and through inspiration. Connecting with nature and being near water tend to intensify spiritual abilities for twelfth house people. Below I am going to discuss some key twelfth house spiritual gifts.

Intuition

Twelfth house people tell me they knew about things before they happened but often ignored that first gut instinct. The ability to sense the truth about situations and other people is a gift. If planets are in the twelfth house, you need to trust your feelings and insights. Pay more attention to the emotions, thoughts, and images that come into your mind. Do not ignore these messages because they are often showing you what is really happening in your life. Intuition is something that can protect twelfth house people from being hurt. It also helps you understand what others are going through and enhances empathy. Using your intuition can help you find solutions to many problems.

Psychic Dreams

One of the most amazing gifts that twelfth house people have is the ability to dream. The twelfth house rules the subconscious mind which is connected to the spiritual realms. You need good sleep to rest the mind each night. During sleep we enter into another world and into deep mystical realms. Dreaming is a way for twelfth house people to gather intuitive messages and information about day-to-day life that helps prepare them for the future.

It is important to pay attention to dream symbols and messages. Deeper information is hidden behind the symbols, and by paying more attention, dreams can reveal the future. Dreamwork will come naturally for twelfth house people. It is an excellent tool for connecting with your psychic abilities and builds greater self-awareness. Keeping a dream journal next to your bed trains your subconscious mind that you are open to remembering. Writing your dreams down every night even if it's just the symbol names, feelings, and energy of the dream will help you remember. Jotting down everything you can remember before waking up will help keep the dreams fresh in your mind so you can analyze them. If you wait too long, you will slowly forget.

Twelfth house people are born with a spiritual awareness that breaks through in dreams and many share with me that they dream vividly. I have never met a twelfth house person who did not have an active dream world. Dreaming of the future can help prepare you for future change and life events. The soul speaks to you through dream images. Dreams are signals of the potential energies coming into reality and reveal life situations that may happen in your life. Dreaming is something that twelfth house people do best. Many twelfth house people experience lucid dreaming, which means they wake up within the dream and realize they are no longer dreaming. The mind awakens during the dream experience.

Clairvoyance

The ability to know or see future events is called clairvoyance. It is also referred to as a sixth sense or inner knowing. Twelfth house people are born with a highly sensitive nature and connect with others on a deeper level. You see what is happening behind the scenes and the subtle issues that others miss. Your gut instincts are never wrong. The still small voice inside your head and the flashes of images are usually right. Trusting yourself is key and this enables you to help others who are in need. Heeding messages that you receive also helps you make better decisions in your life.

This gift is often inherited and there can be a grandparent or a great-grandparent who shares this similar psychic ability. Twelfth house people often see images or flashes while meditating. Writing down what they see can be beneficial. Clairvoyance comes when they sleep and through dreaming. Many twelfth house people dream things in detail before they happen in the real world. Sometimes they just "know" that something is going to happen in the future. When the very thing they knew would happen transpires, they grow more confident in their abilities. It might take time for them to fully trust themselves. Using this ability is important for guiding their life, making the right choices, and trusting the right people.

Automatic Writing and Artistic Abilities

The ability to connect to the spiritual realm and relay information is a special ability. There is something powerful about the connection of the mind, hand, and paper. Writing down words to symbolize feelings is a good way to get in touch with psychic messages. One way twelfth house people can utilize their psychic abilities is through writing. Expressing deep emotions, ideas, thoughts, and experiences can activate psychic abilities. Many twelfth house people have natural creative and imaginative gifts. Writing can be done behind the scenes in private and in seclusion. All these things are comforting for twelfth house people. Grabbing a journal and writing is one technique that helps awaken abilities. It might help to start with a journal prompt or topic which can help get the creative juices flowing.

Allow whatever comes through to be written down without overthinking. Automatic writing is often inspired, like someone or something is sharing information through you. It can feel like you are not sure where these messages are coming from, but you realize they are deep and transforming.

Twelfth house people often have artistic abilities. Many twelfth house clients have shared their inspirational and spiritual art with me. Several artists have been able to bring to life imaginative ideas I had in my mind. The energy of Neptune heightens creative and mystical self-expression. Artistic abilities can manifest in many different ways. One twelfth house person I know combined painting with creating aura photos for others. She travels to different bookstores and draws the colors she sees in her client's energy field. She would psychically sense the colors surrounding a person and then create a drawing for them to keep. Another client would open the akashic records and connect with the client's life seal symbols. She would draw the symbols and bring the images to life and frame it for her clients.

A friend of mine designed the original cover of my first eighth house book. I have a vivid imagination with Sun conjunct Venus in my twelfth. I visualized a phoenix bird rising out of the ashes, there was a tombstone nearby that had the name of a childhood friend who passed away when we were 16, the grim reaper standing there holding a symbol of Pluto, and in the sky an amazing full moon. My friend who has a twelfth house person painted this exact image for me and I have it hanging in my spiritual room. I recently met a wonderful artist who found me through my website. She was an artist studying and obtaining her masters of fine arts degree. She was a twelfth house Sun and has a lot of Pisces energy. I asked her to bring to life twelfth house imagery and an angel. She created an amazing watercolor image that she mailed to me from England. I framed it and have it hanging in my spiritual room. Both eighth and twelfth house imagery were created by two amazing twelfth house artists and

I cherish these works of art.

If you have planets in the twelfth house, you might not even realize that you have artistic gifts. Sometimes these gifts are secretive and kept hidden. It is a blessing having twelfth house planets, and if you make time to express your creative side it can be very healing. You might feel that you are not artistic and doubt your abilities. Be positive and allow yourself to connect with your hidden talents, whatever they may be. Expressing creative energies will help create peace, harmony, and healing.

UFO Experiences

Ever since I can remember I have felt like an alien. I never truly felt that I belonged here on earth. I felt different than everyone around me. As a child I had a fear of being abducted. I never understood where these thoughts and feelings came from. No one ever told me about aliens or extraterrestrials, I just naturally would look at the sky and wonder about life on other planets. I was born with a knowledge of the possibility of life outside our planet. I used to say, "If I see it then I will believe it," and that was my motto. One night when I came home from college my friend and I went for a drive down I-44 highway near my hometown in Missouri. There was a full moon hanging in the sky that night and a clear night full of stars. I was driving and my friend was in the passenger seat. We were listening to music and singing. We were approaching one of the exit ramps and I glanced in the rearview mirror and that is when I saw it.

An enormous saucer-shaped light hung across the entire skyline. I pulled off the exit ramp and parked. I told my friend to look, it's a UFO. We got out of the car. Other cars pulled off and stopped to watch it. We stood underneath this unexplained object. The only way I know how to explain it is that it was like the sky opened up yellow. From one side of the sky, it extended across the highway to the other side. It did not have blinking lights; it was a saucer-shaped yellow light hanging there against the black sky. We watched it for a few minutes, then before our eyes it started shrinking and then disappeared. I have never been able to understand it, but I know what I saw and it was special.

When I started doing astrology consultations in college, I realized I was not the only one who had these experiences. Several clients with twelfth house planets shared with me real life encounters with UFOs, orbs, angels, and lights. Mystical experiences are difficult to explain and many twelfth house people hide them. They are afraid that others would think they were crazy. Twelfth house people often become used to these experiences and they only share them with others who are similar. If you have planets in the twelfth house you are not alone. These experiences are blessings that validate the belief in a higher power.

Chapter Three

Escapism, Detachment, and Addiction & Secrets and Illusions

Escapism, Detachment, and Addiction

I escape in my imagination and when stressed, drink wine because it relaxes me.
– A.U.

Twelfth house energy heightens the need to withdraw from the world of stress and responsibilities. Escaping can sometimes be a good thing and helps twelfth house people recharge themselves. Meditation, for instance, is a healthy way that twelfth house people can escape by connecting within. Other beneficial escapist behaviors could be spending time by themselves reading, writing, watching movies, listening to music, and doing special hobbies.

Imagine feeling all of the emotions, pain, loneliness, and thoughts of others around you. Absorbing everything that is going on in the environment can be overwhelming. The reason the twelfth house is associated with escapism and detachment is because twelfth house people are empaths. They are able to understand people's pain and actually take it on and feel it as their own pain. Many see this ability as a blessing and at times a curse. Finding time to rest and sit in solitude is crucial. Being around people can be difficult and social situations can be draining.

Detaching and escaping from stress comes easily for twelfth house people. Going into their imagination can be a way to withdraw from the world. Escaping through sleep is something many twelfth house people enjoy. I remember being in elementary school and in a class with a teacher who was not very warm or kind to me. I would daydream and zone out the window thinking of adventures I could go on or finding buried treasure in the woods. I would detach from my environment, and when I returned from my deep thoughts, time had passed so quickly. If a subject did not gain my attention, then I would escape into my own inner world.

Some twelfth house people experience feelings of being detached in large crowds. Feeling like being outside their physical body looking in on themselves is common. They feel like reality is a dream and that things are not real. These experiences are heightened by their natural ability to shift their energy out of their body. This experience can happen after going to the movie theater because all of your focus is on the imaginary characters. When you leave the theater, you can feel strange. I have had this happen several times throughout my life. The ability to detach can also become a negative coping mechanism. It can be a way to avoid responsibilities, uncomfortable feelings, relationships, and challenges. It is important for twelfth house people to be in the world but not let the world get into them. Walking in this world with their feet firmly planted on the ground will help them achieve their goals and help them succeed in life. As psychic sponges, people with planets in the twelfth house are known to be hermits. They enjoy isolating themselves. They like to deal with one or two people at a time. They dislike large groups, so small groups are easier for them to feel comfortable in and prevent them from becoming depleted of energy.

Addiction can be a negative part of escapism and many twelfth house people can struggle with addiction. The Neptune influence is strong and influences specific planets in this house as well as aspects to Neptune. Being extra sensitive, caring, and compassionate can be difficult. Overwhelming emotions can lead twelfth house people to find ways to numb themselves. Addiction is a negative coping mechanism and withdrawing from the world brings comfort. In high school if someone cried, then I would cry and feel everything they felt. My way of escaping was not through addiction but by spending time alone shooting hoops, reading, meditating, journaling, and listening to music. Sitting in silence and cuddling with my puppy Rosie always brings peace. I realize how strong the Pisces influence is on planets placed in the twelfth. It heightens psychic abilities, intuition, and empathic abilities more than any other house.

Twelfth house people are kind souls who want to help others feel better and take away their pain. They like to feel needed, and having others depend on them helps them find their soul's purpose. Compassionate and kind, they find a sense of purpose by helping those who suffer. This comes easily because they have suffered themselves and know what it's like. Being a light for others leads to a desire to escape from their own pain. Escaping through alcohol, drugs, work, exercise, and even through food can become a way to cope. Twelfth house people will avoid difficulties by managing unpleasant feelings, thoughts, and emotions in healthy ways.

Secrets, Illusions, and Delusions

When I fall in love, I never see the other person clearly. I see them as perfect.
— J.T.

The twelfth house exists in the area above the horizon just before dawn. The darkness is changing and a glimmer of light breaks through to shine on the dark sky. It is still difficult to see clearly in the morning before the sun rises. This area of life is mystical and spiritual. Things that are vague, hard to grasp, and hard to see reside here. Secrets are associated with the twelfth house, and extreme idealism which can cause illusions. This house is like a mirage, ever changing and morphing our perceptions.

Twelfth house people are known to be secretive, and keep their identity hidden in some way. The energy affects planets placed here by surrounding them with an invisible haze or dusty veil. Sometimes the twelfth house person has trouble even understanding themselves. They often question who they really are and how they feel. This secretive nature manifests as illusive energy to other people which makes it difficult for others to understand you. Others like to project their fears, insecurities, and issues onto you. You might find that you serve as a mirror for those around you. People seem to really love you or dislike you which can be confusing. Twelfth house people often can't see others clearly and this projection issue can cause suffering.

There are different types of secrets that manifest in the twelfth house. The first type are the ones we keep from ourselves. These secrets can lead to self-undoing, which is associated with the twelfth. Anything we do to undermine ourselves is self-undoing. An example would be constantly falling in love and pursuing relationships with partners who are not free to commit because they are already in a relationship. Self-undoing can be both positive and negative. For instance, it can be negative to fall into unhealthy relationship patterns where the twelfth house person is always feeling hurt, abandoned, and used. On the other hand, the positive side of self-undoing can be that these very patterns that are developed are finally recognized and able to be transformed. Great healing and growth come from self-undoing. It is important that twelfth house people recognize what patterns they have concerning self-undoing. Being honest with themselves and being practical about things will help them prevent further difficulties. Many twelfth house people see things with rose-colored glasses and have an extreme idealistic nature. They have good hearts and believe the best in others and often are naïve. Being overly trusting of others can lead to heartache. Living in reality can be difficult for twelfth house people because they are much more comfortable living in their inner world and imagination. Keeping secrets from themselves is easy, like believing the world is a perfect, peaceful, safe place. The ultimate goal is learning to be more practical and grounded.

There are secret talents, abilities, unconscious patterns, and negative personality traits that they are blocked from seeing. They are blind to their own energy and have trouble seeing other people clearly due to an extremely sensitive and emotional nature. Emotions can cloud their judgement. Pain and secrets are often connected when planets are placed in the twelfth. Suffering and sacrifice can go hand and hand with secrets.

The second most common type of secrets are the ones that twelfth house people keep from others. These are the types of secrets they fear will hurt those closest to them. They are very good at pretending and adapting to please other people. Most people open up to twelfth house people because they trust them. People feel their compassionate and kind nature and believe they would never deliberately hurt anyone. This is true. They have the heart of an angel. Twelfth house people do not intentionally set out to hurt others or keep secrets from them. For example, many people with the planet Venus in the twelfth house struggle in matters of the heart and are known to be secretive with sharing how they feel, experiencing clandestine love affairs. This means that they fall in love and might never tell anyone. Sometimes they fall in love with more than one person. They might be married or committed to someone but a karmic attraction leads them into a web of lies, deceit, and secrecy. The secret love life of twelfth house people is often something that could be made into a movie or book. They believe in the motto, "It is better to have loved and lost than to never have loved at all." They often lose at love and have to sacrifice their feelings, life security, and dreams to avoid hurting others. Clients also share with me that they might love someone but keep it secret.

They might go a lifetime repressing, hiding, and avoiding true love.

Secrets Others Keep

People with the Sun in the twelfth house often keep secrets about their identity and personality. Many twelfth house Sun people are born spiritual with some type of psychic ability. They have an interest in supernatural things and enjoy studying new age topics. They might hide this part of themselves from family and friends, especially if they were raised in a traditionally religious household. No one close to them will even know about their secret studies and interests. They are mysterious and illusive to others closest to them. Many twelfth house people have a normal, practical, status quo job where they are successful and hardworking. The other part of their personality shows that they might be an energy healer doing Reiki. They are often found doing tarot card readings, astrology consults, or intuitive readings for those secret few they allow into their inner world. They often live in two different worlds, keeping the appearance of being a certain way to the outside world, but behind the scenes they are very different. They often feel like they don't belong here. They are angels, who were born into the earth realm to walk a special path which is the path of solitude.

The third type of secrets are the kind that other people keep from twelfth house people. Sometimes those closest to them will hide their true nature and motives. Many clients with twelfth house planets have shared with me how they felt let down by people and disliking having to protect themselves from the harshness around them. They shared with me that those they loved the most always seemed to let them down. When they needed help, they never really felt other people were there for them. Trust can be broken easily which causes heartache. The truth is they have to love and care for themselves more than they do for others. They are born givers. Constantly giving people the shirt off their backs, they find it difficult to ever turn down someone in need. Some people will take advantage of that trait and manipulate their kindness.

Many twelfth house people share with me that there are many secrets that their parents kept from them. Secrets involving childhood issues and problems are the most common. There could be mental illness, addiction, extramarital affairs, and even secrets involving paternity. I had several twelfth house clients share with me they found out later in life that the person they thought was their biological mother or father actually wasn't. Some found out they were adopted and this fact was kept hidden from them all throughout childhood. These secrets almost always come out. Twelfth house people are often the last to know about these secrets, living in a dream world. It is not that they are oblivious; they are idealistic seeing things as they want them to be. Because Neptune rules this house it makes it more difficult to see things clearly. There is a mist of illusion that surrounds every aspect of life. Things are masked and hiding in plain sight. Astrologers believe that the closer a planet is to the cusp of the ascendant, the more likely that twelfth house secrets will be exposed. I have found this to be true in my own life and from what clients have shared with me.

Illusion and Delusion

Illusion is like a mirage and many people with twelfth house planets perceive and interpret things inaccurately. They believe in things or people who do not always have their best interest at heart. Delusion is continuing to believe something despite having proof or information that contradicts it. An example would be when a twelfth house person is dating someone and their friends see the lover with someone else. They might even show proof with photos but the twelfth house person will rationalize that it was nothing, maintaining loyalty. The relationship partner is often put on a pedestal. If a partner is being deceptive and hiding things, twelfth house people might not want to believe it. Twelfth house people are good at making excuses for other people's bad behavior. It can be tragic emotionally when they finally see the truth and reality of what is really happening to them. Sorrow, pain, and suffering are associated with the twelfth house because of high expectations. Expectation is everything and twelfth house natives often believe that others are as giving, honest, kind, and empathetic as they are. This is an illusion. Twelfth house people are the kindest, most sensitive, giving individuals in the zodiac. Most people are not born to be angels like they are. They often learn this the hard way, when those people they cared about the most come falling down off the pedestal, shaking up the twelfth house person's entire world. It reminds me of a Netflix show I watched recently, *Tinder Swindler*, about a Casanova con artist who was manipulating kind, caring, and generous women all over the world. The women in the show looked Piscean, Neptunian and had twelfth house vibes. I am really interested to see what is in their natal charts. It reminded me of stories my twelfth house clients have shared with me throughout the years.

Being Practical

It is important for twelfth house people to become more practical and rooted in reality. They are born to live in two worlds, with one foot in the spiritual and the other in the physical world. They have to constantly balance these two separate natures just like the sign Pisces that represents two fish flapping out in the water. There is a dual nature that exists within all twelfth house people. Finding a way to ground themselves in their body will help. Letting go of fantasies and idealism will help twelfth house people see other people more clearly. They often seek a soul mate and many share with me that they believe there is one special person out there for them. They can spend their lives seeking that perfect spiritual connection with another person, but it often ends in loss, heartache, and disappointment. They have to learn to find that love within themselves and realize they are their own soul mate. They can't expect another person to fulfill the void or loneliness they feel inside. They can avoid being taken advantage of when they learn to develop and keep stronger boundaries. When they see something, they need to believe it. One of my favorite sayings I feel is related to the twelfth house is by Maya Angelou. She said, "When someone shows you who they really are, believe them the first time." This saying is helpful in overcoming illusions and believing that people's actions speak volumes.

Chapter Four

Foreign Countries and Large Animals

When I first started studying astrology, I discovered that the twelfth house involved foreign lands and good luck with traveling far away from one's home. I grew up in a small town in Missouri. I never thought I would travel overseas or even meet anyone who lived in a different country. It is amazing how accurate astrology truly is because I ended up traveling all over the world and lived in Germany twice for a total of six years. When I was in high school and college, I never expected that to happen. I remember one time in 1996, I went to a new age bookstore to look for some astrology books. They had a psychic fair going on, I had never been to one before and I felt a little out of place. At that time in my life, I considered myself a Christian mystic and was still a little uncomfortable pursuing all the spiritual interests that I had. It all seemed secretive and taboo at that time and I kept my interests hidden from those closest to me.

Connection to Foreigners

I remember walking over to an older man sitting at a table by himself. He invited me over to do a palm reading for me. I felt excited and really did not believe in palm readings but was fascinated and intrigued. I stuck my right hand out and he held it while he cautiously analyzed it. I will never forget what he said. He told me that I would be known in foreign lands and that I would travel and live in a foreign country away from where I was born. At that time, I had never even left the state of Missouri so it was hard to believe this to be true. He told me I had a connection to Asian culture and that I would have friends from the East. I was excited to hear this but did not know how he could see that from lines on my hand. Palmistry was something I was never really drawn to but I did buy a book to study more about it after this experience. I never imagined that a few years later that I would be in graduate school and doing an internship with international art students from Taiwan, Korea, and China. I was asked to lead a program and develop an international student orientation program. I befriended several students and taught English language classes and basic life skills that the students would need to develop being new to the United States and living in a foreign country. Basic skills like paying rent, ordering off a menu, shopping, and social etiquette were all things I taught them. That year, I won a peer advocate award and have fond memories of the amazing students I worked with. One student I bonded with the most was named Linda. She was an older student in her fifties and was motherly and took me under her wing. She would make me barrettes that were hand painted with beautiful Asian symbols and gave me art that she created. She had her Sun placed in the twelfth like me and I remember her compassionate energy. Wise, kind, and spiritual, she would give me advice and meditate with me.

Living in Germany

In 2000 after being married for one year to my husband who was in the Air Force, we got orders to move to Deutschland— Germany. I had never traveled overseas and had barely been out of Missouri. I remember feeling scared and overwhelmed. Being a military spouse was something new for me and I had never lived more than two hours from home. We moved to Germany and lived in a small village called Bahn outside the main military base in the area near Ramstein. Being new to the country, I wanted to try to learn to speak the language but German was very difficult to learn. I improved and was able to read menus at restaurants and know what the items were but speaking was difficult. Within three years, I traveled to

Austria, Switzerland, France, Spain, Belgium, England, Ireland, Scotland, Italy, Greece, Turkey, Africa, and Egypt. Then again in 2013 we moved back to Germany for a second time and I traveled as much as I could. My mission was to visit as many ancient churches as I could and to travel to sacred religious sites. Ireland was one of my favorite countries. I was amazed by the architecture and art throughout Europe. There were times I felt a sense of knowing and felt comfortable in foreign countries. It was like I had been there before. I experienced déjà vu in Paris and in many places in Italy. I knew what to do and how to travel on the Metro. Looking back, it seems like a dream and like these experiences never really happened. I do believe these international experiences and travels were related to my planets in the twelfth house.

Overseas Travel

Many twelfth house clients have shared with me that they had a restless urge to travel overseas and live somewhere far away. Foreign countries are exotic and there is a secretiveness about them. Many twelfth house people find that their career path leads them to work opportunities and travel overseas. I had a friend with a twelfth house Moon who was able to study abroad for a semester in England. A twelfth house client I helped was able to work in Scotland and live there for a year which was an experience of a lifetime. In my astrology groups on Facebook, I meet people from all over the world who share their experiences with having planets in the twelfth. I have many clients from India with twelfth house planets who reach out to me asking if they will live overseas or have career success in a different country. Twelfth house people are seekers of knowledge and enjoy places that are distant, mysterious, and beautiful. I believe twelfth house people have good luck with foreigners and long distance travel based on my own experiences.

Large Animals

The other interesting thing that the twelfth house is associated with is large animals such as horses, tigers, elephants, and lions. The sixth house, which is the polar opposite house from the twelfth, is ruled by the sign Virgo and is associated with small animals like dogs and cats. When I was growing up, I had two friends who owned horses. I remember riding horses on trails through the woods although I was never very comfortable on a horse and remember getting bucked off a few times. I always thought horses were beautiful creatures. I remember seeing farms nearby where I grew up and there would always be one single horse standing alone out in the grass behind a fence. I remember feeling connected to horses but I never understood why. To me horses seemed like lonely animals and were always by themselves. Looking back, I can see the symbolism and twelfth house connections. I think I was drawn to horses because I always felt alone even when I was with family, friends, or groups of people. There was always this feeling of separateness that I could not quite figure out.

Akashic Records

In 2007, I took a course to learn more about the akashic records. The akashic records are also called the "Book of Life" and are a storage house of information that includes every word, action, feeling, thought, and deed that every soul has experienced. Edgar Cayce was a famous psychic who accessed these records providing insights about health to many people. His readings became deeper where he discussed topics like astrology, Atlantis, aliens, and herbal remedies. Akashic records books and classes are available and are something that many twelfth house people have pursued. To connect with the records, you are taught a sacred prayer. The body and mind must be relaxed and awake to ask questions to pull out images, feelings, and information. Since twelfth house people are connected to the different levels of consciousness, they have a natural ability to open the soul records.

I have always been a visual person with an active imagination, a trait many twelfth house people share. Edgar Cayce was also a twelfth and eighth house person being a Pisces with the Sun in the eighth. He would sleep on his books as a child and wake up and remember all kinds of information. His mind was deep and attached to higher levels of consciousness which he used to help heal others. I open the records for clients before I do their astrological charts. This has helped me see deeper into the life mission and purpose of clients. I share symbolism and try to answer questions using both the akashic records and birth chart. It is pretty amazing how the life seal symbols are very similar to the North Node in the astrological chart of clients. The energy of the records and the birth chart are connected.

When I took my level one akashic records course we practiced as a group and the teacher asked a question about the purpose of the soul. She wanted us to open the records and journal what we sensed, saw, and felt. I started writing and to my surprise my experience involved a horse, which verified the knowledge of twelfth house people being connected to large animals like horses.

March 31, 2007
From the Akashic Records
To tame a wild horse it takes great patience, but also requires the tamer to have a big heart. The horse whisperer speaks in the language of the soul, so the horse knows it is safe and secure. When the tamer speaks in a harsh way, then the horse resists. First you must tame a horse, which means that there is pain and suffering. Difficulties arise when taming a horse because the horse is fighting the master. Once it is tamed the horse can be trained, but not without many trials and tribulations. Being trained means being open to suggestion. When one is open to suggestion one can learn.

The training process is necessary to mend one's wild heart. Just like a horse, the human soul must be tamed by God and then trained, and this is the purpose of our learning here on earth. Through this training the soul grows and heals all the things and reasons that caused it to need to be tamed in the first place. In the end, the horse or soul must learn to submit. It learns submission to its master, who is God. To allow God to work through the soul, there must be these three stages of evolution. They are taming, training, and submission.

Trusting in God's love is similar to the horse's journey and experience. This is why horses are known as one of the most spiritual animals. People believe that horses are lonely animals. They are in many ways because they know they must submit to their master. Who is our master? The one who rides the horse? Who rides us as souls? The answer is God. So, without God, you will always be seeking and fulfilling your loneliness in outside relationships and material possessions.

This information was similar to what others shared and everyone mentioned a horse in what they saw which fascinated me. I do believe that large animals have meaning and there is a reason they are connected with the twelfth house. Many clients have shared with me that they have vivid dreams about specific animals. Animals in dreams represent habits or a part of the personality that is associated with the animal in the dream. For instance, dreaming about a lion symbolizes strength, loyalty, courage, ego, and a desire to be in charge. Twelfth house people may have a desire to own large animals and often horses are the main animal that twelfth house people have a bond with. Equestrian work is very healing and horses are used to help people who have experienced trauma and loss. Horses are used as a therapeutic tool for children with special needs. Larger animals are often exotic and rare just like people who have planets in the twelfth.

In my dream group many share dreams about snakes, spiders,

dolphins, lions, tigers, birds, owls, and bears. When I was living in Germany, I had a vivid dream. It was November 2013 and I was getting ready to start a new job. I was a little nervous about the job and knew it would be challenging. There were a few strong personalities that I was worried about working with. I like peace and did not want conflict.

Snowcapped Mountain Tiger Dream

I went to sleep and had a vivid dream where I was with my husband and daughter in the snow. I looked up and saw amazing snowcapped mountains rising into the sky. We were walking through the deep snow and there was nothing for miles. Suddenly, I looked to the right and saw a large female tiger standing there staring at me. I knew she wanted to talk with me and that I needed to lead my husband and daughter to safety. I watched the tiger and she was waiting for them to leave. They walked down the snowbank hill. I told them to go and I would catch up with them later. I turned to look at the tiger whose eyes were black like obsidian stone. Staring face to face with her I realized something. She was there to warn me. I knew that something was going to happen and I had to be brave, strong, and protective. When I woke up, I experienced strong feelings and knew I had to hang a picture of a tiger in my new work office.

The next day I went to the base exchange to shop and as soon as I walked in there was a painting of a tiger holding its baby cub. I knew that was the picture I needed and purchased it. My first day at work I hung that picture on the wall by the light switch next to the door in my office. I could sit at my desk and see that image to remind me to be brave and strong. A tiger is a powerful animal and I needed to get in touch with my own power. This job challenged me and many difficult people entered my life during that two-year period. That dream still lives in my imagination and I can see exactly what happened in the dream like it was a real memory. I asked my friend who is an artist to draw the dream image above so I could include it in my book.

It is important for twelfth house people to understand how large animals in real life or in dreams can bestow upon them life changing messages.

Chapter Five

Dreaming, Dreamwork, Sleep, and Rest

An unexamined dream is like an unopened letter.
– Talmud

For God does speak again and again, though people do not recognize
it. He speaks in dreams, in visions of the night, when deep sleep
falls on man as they slumber in their beds.
– Job 33:14-16

Sleep is critical for the brain to heal, and without sleep we
would not survive. We need to rest, unplug, and detach
each night before we rise again. Dreams are a part of every
culture. Dreams are one of the most powerful tools we have
to connect to our inner wisdom. In the Bible, dreams are
mentioned 224 times, and there were several key people
who had dreams that gave them signs of the future. Dreams
have always been associated with the twelfth house. I have
never met a twelfth house person who did not have an active
dream world. My twelfth house astrological group had
hundreds of people discussing dreams and how they would
dream things that would happen. I started a Facebook dream
interpretation group to be able to discuss dreams with other
people. Typically, from a young age people with planets in
the twelfth house dream vividly and deeply.

Ever since I was a child I loved to sleep because I looked
forward to my dreams. I kept a journal next to my bed because
my dreams were detailed, long, and like a movie. I bought
dream books so I could look up the symbols in my dreams. I
wanted to learn everything I could about why I was dreaming
certain things and what the symbols meant. I knew my dreams

were guiding me and were signals preparing me for the future. I took all my dreams seriously and paid attention to their subtle symbols.

The unconscious is a twelfth house area. Everything we do in waking life involves our conscious mind. When we rest and sleep, we enter into another state of consciousness called the subconscious mind. The subconscious contains everything that is not stored in our conscious minds. Beliefs, previous lives, memories, skills, and everything that we have seen, thought, or acted on is collected there. It involves inner knowing and is a deep area connected to the psychic world. It reminds me of water and is a translucent area that absorbs everything deeply and is hidden until we bring it to the surface.

The purpose of dreams is to help us solve problems in our everyday lives. Dreams awaken us by helping us grow and become aware of new energy entering our lives. The most important thing that dreams do is warn us, help us assist others, and show signals of potential future events. They prepare us for change. There is a saying that nothing occurs in our lives without first occurring in our dreams. Dreams are reflections of physical conditions, things we repress, subconscious information and super-conscious communication that comes from God.

Concentration

When I was in college, I studied a few years with the school of metaphysics. I was taught a technique called the "candle exercise" that was designed to help students concentrate and focus their mind. This technique was something that we were supposed to practice in order to learn about the power of the conscious and subconscious mind. The goal is to use a tall thin candle and light it in front of you at about an arm's length. You will have paper and pencil nearby and will focus on the candle. Each time your attention is drawn away from the flame you will make a mark on the piece of paper. You will do this exercise for 10 minutes daily. You can see your progress with time and practice. Eventually, your concentration will be stronger than your physical body trying to get your attention. It is designed to help students understand the strength of the conscious mind. It is amazing how your body will itch, twitch, how unexpected thoughts come swirling in, and there is physical discomfort because your conscious mind is wanting your attention. The physical body wants attention and will do anything to distract you. The more you practice, you will find it easier to meditate and still your mind. When twelfth house people learn to concentrate it opens up their spiritual gifts.

Sleep Paralysis, Lucid Dreaming, and Dream Walking

Dreaming is a natural twelfth house gift. Most people with twelfth house planets like to sleep and nap. There is usually a struggle with oversleeping or suffering from insomnia. There are often unexplained experiences that happen in the night right before twelfth house people try to fall asleep. Many clients have shared with me an experience that is often referred to as sleep paralysis or night terrors. An easy way to describe it is that your brain wakes up, but you do not. In Canada they called the experience the "hag effect". This phenomenon happens right before someone is falling asleep or waking up. The person will sense, feel, or see the presence of a supernatural being which immobilizes them. They typically see a person standing at the side or foot of their bed. Some clients share that it is usually a stranger. The person will feel frozen and unable to scream or move but feel they are awake and are aware of their surroundings. They only have control of their mind during this experience.

Sleep Paralysis and Glowing Ball of Light

The first time I experienced sleep paralysis was when I was in high school. I was sixteen years old and was terrified of the dark. I always had to have a night light on and my door wide open in order to see out into the hallway. This unexplained experience was one of the first incidents that I could not explain. After this encounter, I began studying astrology, religion, and dreams to figure out why I had this experience. No one could comfort me or explain to me why this happened. I was on a mission to learn more about myself. After this experience, my intuitive abilities increased and I began dreaming more at night and in more detail. I started keeping a dream journal to document my nightly travels.

I am going to describe exactly what happened that night. The night started off like every normal night before bed. I had just played a basketball game, was wide awake and knew it might be difficult to fall asleep quickly. I read a little bit before bed and then fell asleep. I woke up in the night and looked towards my doorway. I always had the door open so I could see out and there was a night light in my bathroom that I could see. My bed always faced the door which made it easy to see out into the hallway. My parents' room was right across the hall. We lived in a small house and that weekend my father and brother were out of town on a fishing trip.

I woke up in the middle of the night, and when I looked

into the hallway, I saw a glowing ball of light hovering in my doorway. It was about the size of a softball and was yellow but translucent, almost like water. I was scared because I did not know what it was. I tried to scream for my mother but I had no voice. The only thing I had control of was my own mind. I remember praying over and over again, "Please don't have it come in my room." I could not move or speak. I felt paralyzed as I watched this glowing orb float there. It never came inside my room. It took off and went into the bathroom and down the hall and then right back to my doorway. I laid there for what seemed like hours watching it, too afraid to fall asleep. Eventually the force released me, and when I tried to scream, I was able to yell for my mother. She yelled back as I had woken her up. I said, "Look in my doorway, do you see it?" My mother said, "Yes." For the first time I felt validated because someone other than me saw something that was mystical. She told me to go back to sleep, it might be a lightning bug. She kept trying to rationalize it. She even thought someone might be shining a flashlight in the window. I laid there for hours watching it and finally passed out from exhaustion. I regret not getting up and going over to it. I was young, it was the unknown, and during that time in my life I was afraid of my abilities. The next day my mother told me she had no idea what it was and said, "That was definitely not a lightning bug." I told her maybe it was an angel or a spirit guide. I wanted to believe whatever it was wanted to be there for me to watch over me. If I had to do it all over again, I would have gotten up and walked over to it. The lesson learned is not to be afraid. Embrace the unknown and trust your experiences. I believe this was an angel or a spirit guide making its presence known. After this experience I became obsessed with angels and started collecting them.

After this happened, I felt that all my intuitive abilities were heightened and I started having more strange experiences, vivid dreams, and intuitive feelings about people and situations. It is like that experience opened the door to something special inside me. Shortly after this incident I bought my first astrology book and found out that I had the Sun and Venus in the twelfth house. Everything I read was accurate and explained why I always felt so different from everyone and why I had these strange experiences. Astrology opened my eyes and helped me gain greater self-awareness. I would have to say that this glowing ball of light put me on the spiritual path of wanting to understand religion, personality, psychology, and learn ways to help other people.

Psychic Dream and Sleep Paralysis

When I was in graduate school, I had many dreams that would warn me of future events. They were like signals giving me a heads-up. They prepared me for major life changes and emotional upheavals. I remember it was a new semester and I was taking a human diversity class. The first night of class a male student shared some personal information with the class and another student, a girl named Melanie, spoke up and was very conservative and she told him that his lifestyle was against God. I got upset because I saw how hurt this student was and how her words impacted him. I started debating with her about religion. I said to her, "Are you God? How can you judge or say something like that?" We debated back and forth for a bit. I left class upset and went to sleep early because it was late. I had a lucid dream that night in which I was awake. I saw a coffin and the girl in my class. She was crying and coming towards me screaming. I saw the casket, and when I really woke up, I knew it was her mother. My heart was beating fast; I was sweating and the dream felt real. I went back to sleep and had the exact same dream as before, but this time when I woke up something happened. I could not move and I felt a heavy weight on my chest like something or someone was sitting on top of me. I felt this presence and saw a shadow. I could not breathe and felt her mother there with me.

Once I realized what was happening, I yelled and was finally able to physically move off my bed. I turned all the lights on and sat down. In that moment, I can't explain how, but I knew the girl in my class that I argued with was trying to tell me something. I knew her mother died that night after class. I felt it strongly and was emotional. I remember praying and asking for protection. I could not go back to sleep and spent the rest of the night with the light on.

I did not think anyone would believe me if I told them about this death dream but I felt this inner voice telling me that I needed to tell Melanie about the dream. I went to class the next day and she was not there. I knew my dream and experience was a message. Three weeks went by and I asked the professor if she knew where Melanie was and she told me she was not sure she would be coming back. I walked away and felt sad. I wondered why I would dream something like this and never get to see her again. A month after it happened, she returned. I watched her walk in, and she came and sat down next to me. I had not seen her since the night we argued. I looked at her and smiled. I asked if she was doing okay and she seemed caught off guard. She said she was doing fine but she acted strange. I told her I was worried about her and her mother. She then told me her mother died. I will never forget the look on her face. She knew that I knew. She avoided me for a few weeks until summer school started.

We ended up having a death and dying class together which was perfect timing. Both of us were placed in the same group and we had a project concerning rituals of the dead. One day after class she asked if she could talk to me alone. I will never forget that day. We went into the library room and she shut the door. She sat down and looked at me. She said, "I know you knew my mother died. How did you know?" I told her about the vivid dream the night after we had the argument in class, and how when I woke up, I knew her mother had passed. She told me it happened that night but her mother had been struggling with cancer. She got teary-eyed and said to me, "I don't know how you knew, but there is no way you could have known because I did not even tell the professors." I told her that maybe this happened to open up her mind to other spiritual truths and that God is much more than we think he is. She bonded with me and we actually became friends. She even came to my wedding. I felt this dream helped her in some way and I was happy I was able to share it with her.

Sleep Paralysis—Scary Catholic Nun

Most of my sleep paralysis experiences involved me waking up in my bed and looking around, then seeing someone standing there. I would realize I was mentally awake and then scream, and immediately I was back in my body and confused as to what happened. I was unable to hold the experience due to fear. Once I realized I was awake and someone I did not know was standing in my room, I panicked. I would always wake myself up before anything could happen. I do believe I was dream walking. Many cultures believe that when we sleep, we dream in the astral realm and leave our physical body every night. Our soul is attached to the physical body by a silver cord. No matter how far away we travel at night we are always able to find our body again. I think these in between states and experiences occur when the soul is trying to reenter the physical realm. These are just theories, but many twelfth house people have shared with me these exact types of experiences involving sleep and dreams.

When I lived in Germany in 2015, I had a strange experience with sleep paralysis, or the hag effect. I would say this was one of the only times I physically moved across the bed while in this subconscious state. One Sunday we drove to Belgium to a flea market that was very popular. I liked collecting religious icons and unique art. While browsing around I saw something special that I was drawn to. It was a silver crucifix in a wooden frame with red velvet behind it. It matched the color of my bedspread and I thought I could hang it in my bedroom. I bought this unique antique item at this outdoor market. When we got home, I had my husband hang this framed cross in our bedroom. Typically, when I bought antiques, I would cleanse the item but this time I forgot to cleanse it. I went to sleep and woke up in my bed suddenly. I was lying in my bed, looked around, and then when I looked to the right, I saw someone standing there. I closed my eyes and then opened them again. It was dark so I peered closer to see who it was and knew I was awake. I then saw the figure move towards me, and as it got closer, I saw her clearly. It was a short older female nun wearing a full black and white habit. She looked angry and when I realized I was awake, I started screaming. My poor husband was awakened by me screaming and physically moving across the bed. I then "really woke up" and was sitting on top of him. I had moved across the bed to his side just like I did in the "experience". It was real and my mind was fully aware of the experience.

I have never been able to explain this experience. My husband knew it was serious because he heard and saw me act it out. When I woke up, I realized there was something wrong with the antique crucifix picture I had hung up that night. I told my husband to take it down and throw it away. He argued with me and I told him the nun is associated with that item. I wanted it out of the house. He laughed at me but tossed it away anyway. Nothing else happened after that. After that experience, I will never forget to cleanse any antique items.

Glowing Mother

There have been three times in my life when I had the sleep paralysis experience and saw my mother standing at the foot of my bed glowing. All three times after this happened, I reached out to her the next day to make sure she was doing okay. Each time something major had happened and she would be emotionally upset. I have spent many years researching these experiences and I believe they happen to warn me. Maybe I was dream walking and saw her or she traveled to me. It is hard to explain to anyone who has not experienced it. Each time that this experience happened, I woke up in my bed in my own room and realized I was awake. It felt normal because I was in my own bed. Then I looked and saw her. Then my mind started to realize that this was not happening or she should not be here. I panic and get scared and scream. The scream wakes me up for real and I am in my bed truly awake. These experiences are hard to control or hold for very long. Once I scream it ends the lucid experience and I am back in my body. I know I should not be afraid of my mother. What scares me is that I am seeing her standing there and it catches me off guard. Not just seeing a stranger is shocking and unsettling. I can't make this experience happen and it typically occurs out of the blue every couple of years.

Lucid Dreaming

Many twelfth house people have the ability to dream walk and dream lucidly. Dreaming vividly and waking up in your dream, realizing you are awake is lucid dreaming. Sometimes you will have control of the dream, and can tell yourself what you want to happen next and it will. These dreams are very hard to control and hold for long periods of time. The dreamer often wakes up soon after they realize they are dreaming because of panic. Dream walking is common in native cultures and can be done accidentally without trying. It is a practice of sharing a dream with one or more people. Having the ability to enter into other people's dreams and pulling them into your own is a common experience. Twelfth house people are born with several psychic abilities and many dream walkers and lucid dreamers have twelfth house planets. Clients from all over the world have shared with me personal experiences with lucid dreaming and becoming awake within their dreams. Many have the ability to control dreams and change the images. Many clients never realized that there were other people like them out in the world. It's comforting to know that other people have experienced similar things and that you are not alone.

Dreamwork and Clairvoyant Dreams

The twelfth house is the natural place where we can gain psychological information about our inner world through dreams. Some people call it dreamwork or dream incubation. Dreamwork is the study of dreams to gain greater self-awareness, obtain hidden knowledge, and use dreams to heal ourselves and others. Twelfth house people are born to do dreamwork and are natural at documenting their experiences.

They have vivid imaginations that can easily recall dream symbols upon awaking. It is important to write down our dreams and any feelings we have right away. Most psychic dreams or clairvoyant dreams about things coming into our lives or foretelling the future are felt intensely when we first wake up. I have always known when a dream was special and important to listen to. I would write it down but also be able to recall the images and feelings like the dream was a real memory. Many twelfth house clients share similar abilities and a natural desire to dig deeper into their dreams. Some have been healed by their dreams, provided information that saved their lives by listening to their dreams, and changed the course of their future by trusting the messages that came to them at night. Dreams are a powerful source of knowledge that is at our fingertips.

My First Psychic Dream

My first experience of dreaming something before it happened was when I was a freshman in college. A neighbor of mine who I went to high school with still lived in our small town.

I was at my parents' house for the weekend visiting. I went to bed and had a dream about him. In the dream he called me on the telephone and was crying. He asked me if he could come over to my parents' house. I asked what was wrong and he said he would tell me when he came. I hung the phone up. I walked outside and stood on the curb waiting for him. I looked at the sky and there was a full moon. He pulled up in his small yellow car and got out. He had a white T-shirt on, blue jeans, black hat, and glasses. This stuck out because I did not know he wore glasses. He came towards me and hugged me. We sat on the curb outside my parents' house and he told me his parents were getting divorced. He started to cry and we hugged for what felt like hours. Then I woke up. The dream felt vivid and my emotions upon awakening were strong. I wrote the dream down in my journal and went on with my day.

That night I was in my room reading and it was getting late. All of a sudden, the phone rang and when I answered it, he was on the other line. He asked if he could come over and seemed upset. I went outside to wait for him and he pulled up in his yellow car. He slowly walked down the hill. He was wearing a white T-shirt, blue jeans, black hat, and glasses. I remember feeling strange and realized I dreamed this the night before. I watched him come over and I knew what he was going to say. The words came out of his mouth, "My parents are getting divorced." I looked at him and said I know. He was confused. I then opened up to him and shared that I had a dream about him. Everything that just happened tonight was what I dreamed. He did not know what to say. We hugged for hours with the full moon shining brightly in the sky.

This dream experience changed my life. I became obsessed with dream interpretation, research, and trying to figure out why I had dreamed this. The more attention I gave to my dreams, the deeper they became. When I was young, my dreams were like movies and it felt like I dreamed in detail all night. I would keep logs with the date in journals so I would be able to go back and see if I dreamed of a future event. It was my proof and research to show that dreams were messages that guided my life. Dreams have always been an important part of my life.

Dream of Grandmother

The night before my paternal grandmother died, I had a vivid dream about her. In the dream I was awake within the dream and saw her coming towards me. I could not hear what she was saying and she kept trying to tell me something. She was glowing with a light around her. She hugged me and then she faded away. As soon as I woke up, I had a bad feeling.

I knew something was wrong. I told my dad about the dream and asked him to call her. I told him how much the dream about Grandma had bothered me. He finally listened to me and called her later that night to check on her and his sister was there visiting. She said Grandma was doing fine. Later that night, in the middle of the night, my mother woke me up and told me my grandmother had died in her sleep. My parents just got a call from the assisted living facility. It is hard to explain, but it was like she was warning me and saying goodbye. At the funeral, I was able to comfort others because I was calm and peaceful. I was emotionally prepared prior and that made the situation easier for me to handle. Many twelfth house people have shared with me that they have had similar dreams about their loved ones.

Grandmother, Kitchen, and Ghost of Great-Grandmother Dream

My maternal grandmother and I were very close. She was a twelfth house and eighth house person but I did not find that out until I was in college. We would talk for hours and talk about our dreams. When I got married and moved to Germany in 2000, she was upset. I saw her every weekend and now I would be too far away. Once I moved and got settled, we would talk every day on the phone. I would make sure to call her and tell her about my adventures and travels. She was always wonderful on the phone and I never had any concerns until I had a bad dream.

I dreamed I was sleeping in my old bedroom in the house I grew up in. I woke up in the dream and was lying in my bed. I walked down the hallway and turned the corner into the kitchen where I saw my grandmother standing at the sink doing dishes. I called to her but she had her back to me and did not hear me. All of a sudden, the ghost of her mother, my great-grandmother, was coming towards me in the kitchen. She was frantic and glowing white. I started screaming and yelling for my grandmother. She did not respond. I ran over to her and kept saying, "Grandma May is in the kitchen!"

Grandma looked at me and said, "I can't hear you." I was

frantic for her to hear what I was saying to warn her that her deceased mother was in the kitchen. I woke up distraught. I knew when I woke up what the dream meant. I knew that something was wrong with my grandmother's memory. Her mother died from Alzheimer's years ago. Seeing my great-grandmother's ghost in the kitchen and the fact my grandmother could not see her was troubling.

The next morning, I knew something was wrong or something bad was going to happen. I talked to her every day and everything seemed fine. I called my grandfather when I got home from work. The time change made it difficult to get a hold of them sometimes. I told my grandfather that I had a dream about Grandma and that I was worried about her. His voice changed and he seemed caught off guard. He questioned me about what I dreamed. I told him it was not good and I was worried about her memory. He said, "I can't believe this. I have told no one." He went outside to talk and told me that her memory had been getting bad. He could not believe I knew. I told him about the dream and I suggested that she go to the doctor to get checked out. She still seemed fine on the phone but day-to-day memory was affected which he was the only one witnessing. During this time is when she started her slow decline with memory loss which took about 12 years to get serious.

From 2000-2012, I was able to talk with her and she knew who I was. This was a devastating situation for my family and it affected all of us. This dream was a warning for me, and sharing it with my grandfather encouraged him to seek medical advice. It did not change the future or the course of events but this dream was a signal that woke me up to what was really going on with someone close to me even though I was half a world away.

Chariot of Angels and My Grandfather

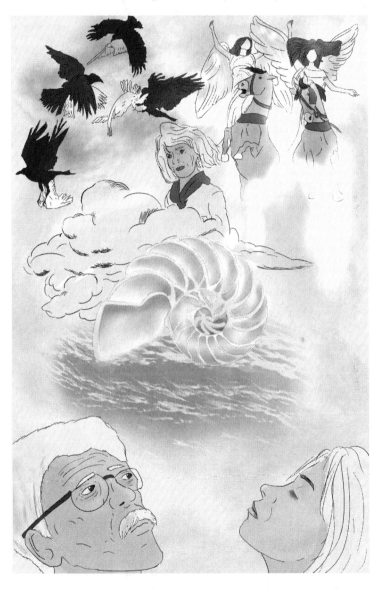

While I was living in Germany in the winter of 2015, I had one of the most spiritual dreams that I have ever experienced in my life occur. I went to sleep and dreamed a movie-like dream about my grandfather. During this time, my mother and grandfather were taking care of my grandmother who was struggling with Alzheimer's disease. It was a difficult time for our family and I felt disconnected from it due to living in a foreign country and being unable to visit her as often as I would have liked. I talked to them on the phone every week and everything seemed fine. In the dream, I was outside with my grandfather. He was shivering and cold. It started raining and dark clouds came rolling in. I saw a tarp and put him under the tarp so he would not get wet. He was uncomfortable and emotional. The rain kept pouring down on us.

All of a sudden, I looked at the sky and saw thousands of black crows flying wildly. I watched them change direction and they all started flying in our direction. I watched them come closer and closer. I stood outside and peered through the rain and saw the crows were clutching something in their claws. When I saw what they were clutching, I let out a shrill scream. The crows were clutching dead white doves in their claws. I yelled and screamed, "No!" I was angry and this was a terrible thing that had happened. Once the crows flew by me, I looked to the sky and saw a chariot of angels coming across the sky riding horses. I felt peace, comfort, and love. The most beautiful music was playing and it sounded almost heavenly, like nothing I have heard before. I could hear the music in the dream, and as I woke up, the music was strongly heard until I fully opened my eyes.

I wrote this dream down in detail. I still remember every single image and feeling that was in the dream. I will never forget this dream. It was foretelling of many things coming into my grandfather's life and my own. That year on December fifth, two months after I moved back to the United States, my grandmother passed away in a nursing home.

Big Bad Wolf and My Puppy Rosie

When I was traveling for work in 2019, I was staying in a hotel in San Diego. I had a dog walker who had been watching my puppy Rosie for about a year. I felt better knowing that she was coming to take care of her while I was away. I went to sleep in the hotel and had a terrible dream. I was in the woods with Rosie. She ran off and I was calling her name. I kept yelling for her and then I saw her in the distance. She was innocently walking around close to a fence. I walked towards her, and as I got closer to her, I saw an enormous life-size wolf standing next to the fence. I screamed to her and she was still walking close to the fence. The wolf had huge claws and it grabbed her through the fence and injured her. I watched it happen in slow motion and started screaming.

I ran to her and she was lying on the ground with a large claw mark on her stomach. I tried to scream and yell for help but I had no voice. I saw people and I kept yelling, "Call 911!" but no sound would come out. I held her in my lap and had blood on my hands. She died in my arms right before I woke up. My heart was beating out of my chest when I woke up. I realized something was wrong. I called my daughter before she went to school and had her do a video call with me so I could see Rosie. She was fine. The dream bothered me all morning. Later that day, the dog walker texted me that she couldn't watch Rosie anymore. The company apparently had not been paying her even though we were paying through the website. It was a long story, but I had to have my neighbor watch her the rest of the week until I returned home.

Black Crow Dream

When I lived in Ohio, I had a strange dream about a glass house. I was inside this house and could see outside. There was a forest with beautiful trees and people were inside the house with me. I walked outside and looked at the sky, and then I saw thousands of black crows flying towards the glass house. The sky was so full of crows that you could not see it or the clouds, only black. I watched the crows fly by me, then in the distance I saw something strange. I saw flashes of red. I focused my vision on the red color and peered through the black crows. Sitting perched on a wooden fence were three red male cardinal birds. I locked eyes with them and knew they caused these crows to come. They stared directly in my eyes and there was something unpleasant about them. I woke up and immediately knew this dream had to do with the Pope and the Catholic Church. That next day when I turned the news on, they were talking about the Catholic priest sexual abuse scandal within the church. This dream was a signal of what was going to happen. For the next year this issue was on the news daily and secrets were brought to light. I believe the crows represented members of the Catholic Church fleeing and leaving. The red cardinal birds represented people in power within the church.

Dreams of September 11, 2001

When I moved to Germany the first time it was in 2000. From the moment we moved there, I started having recurring dreams about airplanes flying into buildings and exploding. I wrote these dreams down in my dream log every night and wondered what they meant. The dream book said airplanes are associated with work and large organizations. This analysis never made sense to me. The dreams kept recurring for several months. Then they changed with me on the airplane instead of watching the airplanes in the distance. One specific dream I will never forget. I was on the airplane and it was getting ready to take off. I looked and saw that Michael J. Fox, the famous actor, was on the airplane with me. I looked up towards the front of the plane and saw some men with guns. I knew the plane was being hijacked. The plane slowly started to prepare for takeoff going faster on the runway. I told everyone that the plane had been hijacked and no one believed me except Michael J. Fox. I said, "We have to get off this plane." He got up with me and we ran to the emergency door and opened it. We jumped out and rolled onto the tarmac. I turned and watched the plane take off and then it turned and flew into two towers and exploded. I woke up with my heart pounding.

A few months later, I was working on an Army base. I was on the phone with a soldier who was in the United States and he told me something happened and that we should turn the news on. I gathered my coworkers and we turned the television on in the meeting room. We watched live when the second plane flew into the World Trade Center. I will never forget that day and the eerie feeling that came over me. I remember telling my husband that I'd had dreams about this for months. I even got my dream journal out and showed him the dated entries. I realized that I had dreamed this multiple times for a whole year. The strange thing was that several of the hijackers were living in Germany not far from where we lived. The news revealed that they were planning this attack while in Germany. I believe a few attended a university in Germany before this happened. Watching it unfold in real life is something that I will never forget.

Japanese Tsunami Dream 2012

When I was living in Virginia, I went to bed one night and found myself floating in the ocean. The waves were violent, crashing up against the rocks. The ocean water was forcing me against the rocks and the waves pushed me underneath the water. I swam down into the ocean and saw dolphins, sharks, whales, and fish going crazy. They were unsettled, floundering under the water, and some were frantic. As I swam up to the surface, the waves were pushing me up against the rocks. I looked and saw the sand and there were dead sea animals all over the shore. The ocean was surging and rough. I kept trying to stay above the water, but the waves were powerful and hit me hard against the rocks. When I woke up, I had a bad feeling. I knew something was going to happen to the ocean. I walked downstairs and my husband asked me if I had seen the news and he told me there was a tsunami in Japan. I looked at the television and saw the images. I almost tripped and felt nauseous. I told him that I had just dreamed about this last night. I will never forget that day. This dream was vivid and still sticks in my mind like a real memory.

Flying and Dolphin Lucid Dream

A few months before the coronavirus pandemic hit the world, I had a strange dream. I dreamed I was flying fast above the ocean water. As I was flying, I looked in the distance and saw a strange-looking bridge that went across the water. Then I saw a dolphin jumping up out of the water. While flying, I became lucid and realized I was dreaming. I could feel the air, and mist of the water hitting my face. I started to panic because I knew I was awake and I started going down closer to the water. I did not want to hit the water so I intentionally told myself to go to the bank. I flew over to a green patchy area covered in beautiful flowers. I woke up right away. Later, I was watching the news when they were showing China and

I saw the bridge that was in my dream months before.

Twelfth House Dreams

I wanted to share some of my twelfth house dreams because many clients with planets in the twelfth share similar experiences. These dreams changed my life. Dreams have changed the lives of many people. There are too many dreams to include in this book but I wanted to share a few with you. Most twelfth house people have shared similar types of dreams with me; amazing, vivid, imaginative, transforming, mysterious dreams that shaped the future and protected them from harm. Dreams have a large impact on the lives of twelfth house people specifically because it's like they have a guardian angel watching over them. They are guided by their dreams and believe in the insights they give.

Universal Dream Symbols

The 10 most common dream symbols according to *dream.com.uk* are listed below.

1. Teeth falling out
2. Flying
3. Falling
4. Being chased
5. Being naked
6. Failing exams
7. Being late
8. Unable to find a toilet
9. Driving
10. Finding an unused room

Twelfth house clients share with me that they often dream of deceased loved ones, flying, death, and animals. Every dream symbol is important and has an energy that exists behind it. To understand what the dream is saying, you have to dig deeper to understand the message. Symbols can mean different things for different people. For instance, dreaming about a dog can mean different things depending on if you like dogs or if you are afraid of them. Animals represent habits and dogs are sometimes associated with loyalty, man's best friend, and companionship. Dreaming of death often represents change in our lives. It can be scary to dream about someone dying but it often is symbolic. We will discuss dream interpretation and ideas for dream journal prompts in the next section.

Dream Interpretation

Many dream books discuss theories on dream interpretation. Some basic things are the belief that everyone and everything in the dream represents you or an aspect of yourself. I believe this is true for normal dreams but for twelfth house people, our dreams tend to be deeper and even more profound. Twelfth house dreams are spiritual and often carry psychic messages within them. Some of my dreams are normal dreams and the symbols can be analyzed with the basic method. Although, several dreams that occur every year for me are not easily analyzed and no dream book could help me find the meaning. I had to do a little more digging and self-reflection to figure out what resonated with me. These clairvoyant dreams that predict the future or what is coming into life are often harder to interpret at the time we have them. This is why keeping a dream journal is so important because it enables us to go back and read what we dreamed. This validates our life experiences and we can begin to see how we are warned of many things through the dream process. There is a force trying to give us insight and even protect us by giving us dream warnings. It does not matter if you call it God, angels, or the soul. There is a destiny and purpose to life on earth and some events are meant to happen regardless of what we do. This is why I have learned to believe in destiny. I have seen too many things not to believe. This is one twelfth house blessing, the gift of belief.

Signs and symbols in a dream typically mean exactly what they are saying. Sometimes we dream of things that only we would understand. Dreams can relate to the same problem, and many believe right before we wake up, those dreams are the most spiritual messages. First try to be practical in your interpretation and ask yourself if it relates directly to something in your life. Trust yourself and your interpretations. Do you continue to dream about the same themes in all your dreams? Look back and compare your older dreams with your newer ones to see if there are connections. Always try to assess how the dream makes you feel and if anything in your life could be affecting the images you are dreaming about. Figure out if you are struggling in relationships, with work, parenting, or with health issues that could be themes repeating at night trying to get your attention.

It is easier to interpret a dream when we connect with the energy behind the symbols. There was a process I learned during metaphysics classes that helped me interpret my dreams. The technique is called process psychology and was developed by Arnold Mindell. He theorized that humans have a dream body. He believed the relationship between our dream images and our physical experiences is what helps us get in touch with our dream body. This method can be used to become more connected by tapping into our subconscious energies. The below exercise can be used to gain deeper understanding of your dreams.

Experiential Exercise (From Arnold Mindell Process Psychology http://www.aamindell.net/dreambody)

1. Sit relaxed in a quiet place where you won't be disturbed.
2. Take 10 deep circular breaths connecting the inhale with the exhale in a big circle.
3. Bring your awareness to your physical body and any

area, feeling or problem you are currently having.

4. Any symptom or sensation that comes up for you, feel it as exactly as you can. Just feeling it is important. Feel it and increase or amplify it. Feel the pressure, the temperature, the location and extend where it is, and experiment with a small feeling or sensation throughout your whole body; you may want to close your eyes to go further inward to your sensation.

5. As you feel it more, make a picture of the feeling you're having in your imagination, not a general picture, but a picture that represents the particular feeling that you're having in your body right now. Take your time. Then allow that picture to unfold as if you were at the movies. While you let the picture unfold, internally watch the scene go on in your imagination. If it begins to slow or stop just go back to amplifying whatever is there in your body or your movie scene. If someone or something is doing something in your movie, amplify it by having them do it more!

6. Now, ask yourself, "Have I recently dreamed in the last few days, weeks or months something like the picture that I am now seeing?" Have you ever seen such a picture before, or one that is similar or somehow associated with it? Have you dreamed about figures who do the same thing as the ones in your present picture?

7. Can you connect this with an experience in your everyday life?

8. For those who wish to continue, make a movement that goes along with the particular body feeling you were having. Physically move and express the feeling and visualization you had before.

9. Notice the movement you are making and let it move more to complete itself. Amplify it.

10. Have you noticed or do you remember that movement

in the past? Has it been trying to appear before in your life? You probably make it a lot spontaneously, which means it has been a movement asking for expression and integration in your life. As you follow it and allow it to unfold, you'll put together pieces of incomplete movements and body sensations and dreams and relationship interactions into one big whole expression that spans many life experiences.

Continuing to breathe with connected, circular breaths helps to keep the process flowing. As your breath flows, so flow the energies and emotions.

Tips for Remembering Dreams

The first step in remembering dreams is to set your intention. You must first ask your subconscious mind to assist you in remembering. Before you go to sleep, make sure you have a dream journal and pen sitting next to your bed. It is helpful for me to put the date each night. I also write down if there is a full moon or if I am on my menstrual cycle etc. Pray for guidance and ask the universe to give you messages in your dreams. This starts the muscle memory in your levels of consciousness that will help in recall. Try to write down whatever you remember immediately upon awaking before you move your body. Jot down names, images, symbols and feelings in your journal. Even if it is the middle of the night, I lean over and write down the key symbols and messages. Then when I wake up fully in the morning, I write down more details of what I can remember. It is also important for twelfth house people to get enough adequate sleep that includes deep levels of rest. Balancing the body, mind, and spirit is important in reducing stress and this will increase dream recall. Medications can disrupt dreaming and when I have taken Ambien, I do not remember my dreams at all.

When I take melatonin, my dreams are more vivid and a little strange.

Meditation can help enhance our ability to dream. It helps calm the mind, and reduces stress. Detaching from the physical realm also helps us break down barriers between the conscious, subconscious and superconscious mind. This practice integrates different parts of the mind which helps in dreaming. The more you practice and put effort into remembering dreams the more likely you will begin dreaming. Very few twelfth house people have difficulties dreaming or remembering dreams, but if you have difficulties, you can utilize these tips.

Some things that block us from remembering dreams are lack of interest, being overly focused on material things, physical and mental exhaustion. Medications and other impurities in the physical body can make it difficult to remember dreams.

Dream Journal Prompts

1. What symbols were in the dream?

2. What do you think the symbols mean?

3. What feelings did you have upon awakening?

4. What is the theme of the dream? Is there a plot?

5. How does the dream turn out?

6. What do you think the dream is trying to tell you?

7. Did the dream or parts of it happen in real life? Was it prophetic?

Sleep and Rest

I need sleep to function in this world, to wake up and go to work. I need more sleep than anyone else in my family.
— Female, U.S.A.

Getting enough sleep is crucial for twelfth house people. They tend to be night owls, staying up late and sleeping in. Many people with twelfth house planets tell me they are not morning people. They often do their best work late at night when things are quiet and everyone else in the world is asleep. They are known to use sleep as an escape, especially when they are feeling stressed and anxious. Sleeping too much or experiencing insomnia are both common for twelfth house people. Taking short naps for 20 minutes can help recharge their energy. Ensuring that they have a set bedtime schedule and ritual will help keep their sleep rhythms balanced. If their sleep becomes disturbed, they can struggle with irritability, frustration, depression, and are known to take out their negative emotions on those closest to them. Routine is key and helps alleviate exhaustion. Sleep is known to heal the body and mind. The brain shuts off and recharges itself when we enter the different stages of sleep.

Withdrawing from the world and taking time to rest is like heaven for twelfth house people. Resting means doing nothing strenuous. Activities that benefit twelfth house people are meditating, reading, watching television, writing, and doing nothing. Taking a break from practical duties and the real world can be relaxing for them. Making time to do nothing and rest helps them refill their energy tank. They need time for sleep and rest because it helps them feel reinvigorated and prepared to go out into the world again. They should make these things a priority. It will help them serve others who need them when they are out in the world.

Chapter Six

Sun & Moon: Karma with Father and Mother & Developing Boundaries

Sun & Moon: Karma with Father and Mother

My mother needed my help and I felt like the mother figure.
– A.S.

When people are born with the Sun placed in the twelfth house of the birth chart there is learning surrounding the father figure. The father figure is often absent or missing from the life. There can be feelings of an absent connection or bond even if the father is around. Twelfth house Sun people are meant to seek a connection with a higher power. They have to learn to develop a spiritual path and to make that a priority in their life. When they learn to do this, they will have many blessings. Sometimes the father figure can struggle with depression, alcohol addiction, or due to parental divorce, does not have a strong presence in the twelfth house person's life. Many twelfth house Sun people benefit from someone older and wiser such as a grandfather. There are many blessings with this placement and difficulties to overcome. Born to help others, twelfth house people have to learn to love themselves and give themselves energy, time and patience. The key to happiness is to treat themselves how they would treat others. They are born givers, but don't always know how to do self-care.

When the Moon is in the twelfth, you often have a strong attachment and bond with your mother figure. The relationship with your mother can become unhealthy at times and cause a lot of pain. You might feel like you have to be responsible for your mother's well-being and take care of her. The child and parental roles are often switched with this placement, with the Moon person feeling like they are the parent. The mother figure and female influences in your life teach you a lot about spirituality and metaphysics. There could be a spiritual gift passed down from generation to generation such as psychic abilities, clairvoyance, and psychic dreams. Mental health issues can affect the mother's life in some way such as depression, anxiety or past trauma. Unlike the Sun, the Moon in the twelfth house can signify enmeshment issues with the mother and not the absent bond we find with Sun in the twelfth. You will want to take care of your mother physically and emotionally but will need to develop healthy boundaries in order for it not to hurt your life.

Some of the greatest karmic lessons are learned from our parents. Twelfth house people have high expectations and unrealistic beliefs about how our parents should be. It is important to remember that parents are human and going to make mistakes, no one is perfect. Some spiritual teachings believe that our soul chooses our parents before we come into the material plane. Our true parent is God, and when we see our parents are souls who are learning lessons just like we are then we are able to forgive them for their mistakes.

Developing Boundaries

When we fail to set boundaries and hold people accountable, we feel used and mistreated.
— Brené Brown

Twelfth house people often struggle to protect themselves from other people's energy. Pisces traits are enhanced when planets are placed in the twelfth. Lack of boundaries and strong empathic abilities create a highly sensitive nature. Twelfth house people absorb everything going on in the environment which can lead to feelings of depression, anxiety, negativity, and exhaustion. They often feel drained after interacting with people at all, especially in large groups of people where they are forced to socialize. Benefits and strengths come from developing a thicker skin. Boundaries help twelfth house people protect their own thoughts, emotions, and feelings. It is important that they ask themselves, "Is this mine or someone else's energy?" Distinguishing between their own feelings and the stress they have absorbed in the world is key to connecting to who they really are. People with problems, pain, and troubles are attracted to people with planets in the twelfth house. Twelfth house people are like candles whose light shines bright and attracts all lonely, hidden, and wounded people and situations. The dark is always drawn to the light. People with dark personality traits, ulterior motives, secret enemies, selfishness, and opportunists come to them for help. Twelfth house people burn out because they find it difficult to say no to others. They dislike hurting people's feelings. The lack of boundaries and the inability to stand up for themselves can cause problems. They often neglect themselves by always putting other people first. Overcoming this trait is a major step in focusing on self-care.

Twelfth house people serve as mirrors for others. They reflect what others feel and vice versa. They often reflect their own feelings onto others and only see what they want to see. Being reflectors, they walk around feeling let down by how others disregard them and their emotions. They mirror back to others their unconscious personality traits and emotions. Other people can feel vulnerable and exposed around twelfth house people. I remember the first time I realized there was something about me that others liked but there was also something about me that made some people feel very uncomfortable. When I studied psychology and astrology, I realized that I was reflecting to others issues they needed to confront. People either loved me instantly or disliked me and made it known. When I was sitting in class or around large groups of people, I would visualize a mirror around myself. This was a way to protect myself from absorbing everyone's thoughts and feelings. I was super sensitive and needed protection. This imaginary mirror in my mind would help me feel invincible and sheltered from the negative energy around me.

Twelfth house people are selfless, compassionate souls who want to take on the pain of the world to ensure other people feel better. They need to remember they don't have to be a martyr. Having healthy boundaries is natural and is not selfish. They have to shift the focus on themselves so they can have the strength to help others who deserve their help. A big challenge is to stop giving their energy to people who only take from them. Twelfth house people will feel healthier, stronger, happier, and more energized when they develop healthy boundaries. They will be capable of living in the world with their feet firmly planted on the ground.

Chapter Seven

Suffering, Empathy, and Compassion

I was always sensitive, emotional, and concerned about others. When someone was sad, I would feel it. When someone cried, I cried with them. I would feel other people's emotions like they were my own. I never understood why I felt things so intensely. I remember thinking there was something wrong with me. I felt different from all my friends and other people my age. I remember people telling me I was too nice and that I let people take advantage of me. I never understood why I would go out of my way to help other people. The students that no one else would talk to, I would talk to them. I was intuitive and could sense when someone was lonely. I tried to make other people feel better. It hurt me to see someone struggling or being bullied. I did not like feeling strongly about things but I could not control it. I was wide open emotionally and my heart was vulnerable. I remember having my feelings hurt very easily, too easily at times. I had no protection to guard my inner being from harshness, cruelness, and heartlessness. I did not understand how people could hurt others without any care in the world. I watched how people treated each other badly and sometimes people did the same to me. Those situations were learning experiences and helped me realize that I can't trust everyone.

When I started studying astrology at the age of 16, it stemmed from that unexplained experience of seeing the glowing ball of light in my doorway. I bought my first book and realized I had the Sun and Venus in the twelfth house. I remember reading the words compassionate, spiritual, kind, and someone who has mystical experiences they can't explain. I knew there was truth in astrology and I was hooked. I had to find out more about it and myself. Astrology became my passion because it validated my inner feelings. It validated my experiences and personality on a deeper level. I began to accept my abilities, intuition, feelings, and desire to help those who were suffering.

Twelfth house people are meant to serve or suffer. As long as they help others in some way their life improves. It is part of the spiritual mission of this house to force us to feel other people's pain so we can try to do something about it. When planets are placed here there will be special talents, but hard lessons to learn. Selfless service is the best way for twelfth house people to overcome obstacles. Positive life experiences and good luck come their way when they help others. Everything they do comes back 10 times stronger even though it might seem like it takes a long time to happen. Typically, they are angels helping others, and it is rare for them to have anyone offer the same kind of assistance. This is why they often report feeling lonely.

Feeling compassion for those less fortunate comes naturally. Suffering is associated with this house because by feeling pain twelfth house people are able to grow stronger spiritually. They learn to depend on themselves and a higher power. Empathic abilities can be a blessing and a curse. Feeling everyone's emotions on top of being hurt easily leaves them vulnerable. Wearing their heart on their sleeve can set them up to be hurt by others who do not understand how fragile they are. Twelfth house people have high standards and strive to be perfect. No one is perfect and we all make mistakes. They struggle when they fall short of how they feel they should be. Loving and accepting themselves is crucial. People with planets in the twelfth house are the most compassionate people I have ever met. They are amazing listeners and truly put themselves in other people's shoes. The twelfth house motto is the classic, "Treat others how you want to be treated," or the golden rule. Jesus spoke so clearly about this in many parables. Buddha taught a similar teaching known as karma. Twelfth house people are natural at giving and live by this motto. Twelfth house people's energy and capacity for compassion is heightened to levels that normal people can't attain. If you need someone who truly understands your pain and cares, find another twelfth house person to talk to.

Chapter Eight

Romanticism, Heartbreak, and Love Lessons

Searching for a soul mate, experiencing romantic feelings and heartbreak are all twelfth house lessons. Many clients have shared with me that loss of love and heartbreak is one of the most difficult things they have experienced. Intimate relationships can be challenging for twelfth house people. They have to learn to be more practical in love. The energy of Neptune sprinkles a cloudy mist around them making it difficult to see other people clearly.

They are known to sacrifice themselves for those they love. Extreme romanticism can happen with any planet in the twelfth but especially the Sun, Venus, and Mars. Attracting people who need help or have pain can become an unhealthy pattern. High expectations and illusions can set them up for disappointment. When the people they idealized turn out to be dishonest, opportunists, or emotionally unavailable, they are left to pick up the pieces. They have a tender, compassionate heart that loves deeply and has trouble letting people go. They feel sorry for people even when they shouldn't; it's a good trait but it can cause them a lot of pain. Twelfth house people can't change others no matter how hard they might want to. Believing the best in everyone is something they do well.

Ever since I can remember, I was emotional and wanted to find someone to love. I would imagine and visualize the perfect romantic partner. Just like the movies I watched, I believed that true love existed. Finding a soul mate was always on the forefront of my mind when I was growing up. All my serious relationships in high school were long-term. My first boyfriend was two years older than me and we spent every waking moment together. My life revolved around him and if we were not together it felt like something was missing. I joined him on hunting and fishing trips with his friends. I remember listening to the band Chicago and replaying their love songs on my Walkman before basketball games. Even though I was a Virgo Sun Sign, I always felt like a romantic Pisces. It all made sense when I found out I was a twelfth house person. My identity was connected to and impacted by love relationships.

The greatest pain I have ever experienced was from relationship partners. My emotions were strong and obsessive. Because all of my relationships were long-term, it was always difficult for me to move on. I did not let go easily or forget. I learned many lessons in love by feeling abandoned and discarded. Abandonment in relationships creates deep wounds. Healing uncomfortable feelings concerning love, romance, and intimacy will help twelfth house people trust others. Losing someone you love because they simply don't love you anymore can be painful and many twelfth house people experience this. Unrequited love, just like in the movies, is something twelfth house people live through and it's often more than once.

Many twelfth house people believe in twin flames and soul mates. They spend much of their life looking for connections but they are with the wrong types of people. Love can be experienced and felt in many different ways. Some believe it involves friendship, loyalty, passion, sexual intimacy, and trust. Chemistry can be fleeting but true soul bonds are everlasting. When you feel a connection with someone and it feels like you have known them forever, it is often from a past lifetime. Twelfth house people have relationship karma and attract many souls that they loved before. This can be challenging as there are often many painful debts to pay. The universe seeks balance. I have come to believe that when there is a strong, immediate attraction, then twelfth house people need to be cautious. There are often unhealed issues that have to play out, and it does not always end well.

Twelfth house clients believe that love can conquer all

and these idealistic beliefs can cause pain, suffering, and disappointment. Past experiences can cloud their vision and make it difficult to trust others due to past hurt. Giving their loyalty, heart, and soul on a deep level can put them at risk for experiencing betrayal. It is part of life and everyone gets hurt sometimes but they take it harder than most. Twelfth house people have to learn to love themselves just as much as they love others. Ending one-sided relationships will make them stronger. Pouring energy into themselves encourages self-care because the natural energy of the twelfth is to give energy.

Valuing and accepting their own flaws are lessons that have to be mastered. Balancing how much energy is given away, developing boundaries, and believing they deserve love are the first steps in healing twelfth house energy. Reciprocation in relationships is a must and they should not tolerate anything less. True love is proven by actions not just words. People who support twelfth house people like family, friends, and loved ones are the people who deserve support in return. Many people are not on the same level spiritually, emotionally, intellectually, or soul wise. They can't love unconditionally like twelfth house people do. Twelfth house people need to realize how lucky they are. They are destined to find true love within themselves. Connecting to a higher power and feeling love that is beyond the physical realm is their reward.

Chapter Nine

Invisibility, Secret Enemies, and Hidden Talents

The influence of the planet Neptune, the natural ruler of the twelfth house, has a major impact on feelings of invisibility. Neptune is the culprit and reason why twelfth house people often feel unappreciated and ignored. Twelfth house people often experience disappointment because they feel like they never get recognized for their good deeds or talents. I have felt this way before, all of us have, but for twelfth house people it is more profound. There have been times that my accomplishments or good deeds were completely ignored. There were many times that others would take credit for my ideas and work. When this happened, I would feel frozen and unable to even say a word. Part of it was shock and never expecting other people to do something like that. I started hearing similar stories from many people with planets in the twelfth house. Many expressed experiences of feeling invisible or experiencing others ignoring them like they were not even there.

Twelfth house people are special and here on this earth for a specific mission and purpose. I am often tested in my own life with expectations. I have felt let down, taken for granted, and unappreciated most of my life. When I finally realized that these feelings were meant to be in order for me to transform into an unconditional servant, this is when I healed these emotions. Helping others selflessly without a need for reciprocation is the lesson. Selfless service means we get satisfaction from within ourselves. I think part of the problem for me was that my love language is words of affirmation. I feel loved when I hear people share words of appreciation and communicate with me. The strong Virgo in my chart enhances this need. I realized after having my feelings hurt time and time again, there was something different about me. How I expected to be treated was not how others would treat me. To me, it seemed so simple and easy. I did not understand why others continued to let me down emotionally. Family, friends, and coworkers would seem to just expect me to give without reciprocation. I realized part of this lesson is about developing boundaries. I could go long periods giving and was inspired by knowing inside my heart that I was helping the lives of others. Twelfth house people can go months and even years serving without exhaustion, but one day they can feel burned out. It happens to us all. As I said, I like the saying, "You can't pour from an empty cup." We have to fulfill ourselves and replenish our own spiritual energy to continue to serve selflessly as we are destined to.

As twelfth house people, we have to learn self-love and be able to give ourselves the appreciation and acknowledgment we are looking for outside ourselves. Connecting to spirit and a higher power is the fastest way for twelfth house people to heal these unpleasant feelings. Meditating, relaxing, writing, and sitting in silence listening to uplifting music can all bring comfort and the strength to overcome feeling invisible. Other people's appreciation will never satisfy us because it's worldly. Twelfth house people are not from this world. We walk in the energy between worlds. Therefore, we feel invisible and, in a way, we are. Our soul and essence are not fully here on earth or in our physical bodies. We detach and daydream, living in our imagination and in the akashic realms.

Recently I had this test of feeling invisible pop up again in my life. I had multiple experiences of people not seeing me. I was on a zoom session for a course I was helping teach for work. I put a lot of time and effort into helping teach this two-week class. On the final day of the class, the lead was introducing all the faculty. They introduced everyone and allowed them all to talk, except they forgot about me. I was on camera waiting but not acknowledged. This kind of thing happens to me all the time and I know it's my twelfth house Sun energy. I said to myself, "Am I invisible or something?" I even tried to talk at certain points, but others talked over me and it was like no one heard me. They never introduced me but that same week I had other strange things similar to this happen. This is when I realized the truth of twelfth house feelings of invisibility and a few people in my twelfth house Facebook group posted similar experiences.

Even at work, I will be in the office and someone will say, "Oh I did not realize you were here; I walked by several times and did not see you." I am thinking to myself, "That is strange because I have been here the entire time and watched you walk by ignoring me." There are many times when I will be in a room with a group of people and it's like they can't see me or acknowledge my presence. As a Virgo, I am modest and do not like to be exposed or in the limelight, so it is something deeper going on and I feel I just want others to see me. We are invisible to many, but those who need us will find us. The people meant to seek our help and those with pain find us easily. I used to say, "I must have a sign on my back that says come to me if you need help." I have felt this way my entire life. Now at age 46, I still feel that most people only talk to me if they need something from me. I still feel that I don't get credit for the work I do. I still feel people take my kindness for granted and even try to manipulate me. These relationships are evident in my life and leave me feeling sad and let down. I withdraw from people easily now when I experience this energy, I see them clearly now that I am older. I have heard several twelfth house people share stories about this in my groups. Sometimes they share with me that they had an idea or project at work that took off and was successful. The next thing they know, their coworker, who did nothing to help but is good at bragging about themselves, takes credit for the project in front of management and supervisors. Others are rewarded and highlighted for the job you did. This happened to me a lot throughout my career. The sad part is that it was usually done by someone I trusted and considered a friend. We know the truth inside our hearts and that should be enough. It's human nature to want to be recognized and appreciated. I always wondered why other people believe these things and do not see the clear truth. Feeling betrayed by those we did so much for can leave us feeling empty, sometimes like a victim. Our kindness sometimes seems like an invitation to take advantage of us and it's like people know we will forgive them so they continue to do these hurtful things. We often ask ourselves, "How can they not see that their behavior was wrong?" Understanding other people's behavior can be difficult and impossible at times. I realize there is a lot of unresolved anger inside twelfth house people because we feel it's not appropriate to be angry. I want to say it's absolutely necessary to feel anger, and to understand that underneath that anger is often hurt.

The lesson here is that we have to let go of a need for recognition, acceptance, and appreciation. When we truly release the ego desires and all the Neptune idealism, high expectations, and illusions, then we start to feel lighter. When we truly let go, guess what happens? We receive an acknowledgment from the universe. Something positive will happen to us and we get a sense of justice. It might take time, but be patient, it will happen. The twelfth house is after all the house of guardian angels. Believe me, angels are watching over twelfth house people and protecting them even if they can't see them. Your light shines so brightly that most people are blinded by it. When the light is so bright people can't see us at all. This is why it's like we are invisible. It's not our fault. We are just being ourselves. It is often those with a bright light or larger light than our own who recognize us and make us feel seen for the first time. Twelfth house people are lights in the darkness and attract people, and if we can remember the deeper reason why then we will embrace this gift. The gift of discernment, compassion, wisdom and selflessness are things we can strengthen.

Secret Enemies

Secret enemies and their association with the twelfth house have always fascinated me. I have found that sometimes twelfth house people are their own worst enemy. They allow others to hurt them by the lack of boundaries they possess, by being timid, avoiding conflict, and a fear of hurting other people's feelings. Being selfless and sacrificing for others can also make them their own worst enemy. I find that many twelfth house people have felt betrayed by someone they trusted. All human beings have experienced this but the twelfth house is a special place. My research shows that twelfth house people often are extraordinarily sensitive, kind and emotional. They have high expectations of others like we discussed before. Believing others are similar to them makes them expect a certain outcome from others. When they are let down, hurt, and disappointed by others they cared about, this causes them to feel betrayed. It takes a long time for them to trust others again. This can make them feel like they have secret enemies. Just like Judas who betrayed Jesus with a kiss, twelfth house people often feel that they are hurt by those they loved the most.

Twelfth house people serve as mirrors for others. Sometimes the greatest enemy is us, but we don't always see it. The self-fulfilling prophecy of believing that others are only out to hurt us can become a belief system based on past experience. Negative thoughts, emotional patterns and expectations can create the feeling of having secret enemies. In reality many troubles that twelfth house people have come from their own energy. In many of my astrology groups the question about secret enemies and the twelfth house is always asked. I see it manifest both ways.

There are times twelfth house people are hurt by those closest to them like family and friends. Then there are times that their own patterns get them into difficult situations.

Secret enemies can cause a lot of confusion, chaos, conflict, and dysfunction in the twelfth house person's life. People hidden away in prisons, hospitals and foreign countries can manifest in your life. There are many stories twelfth house people have shared with me about shocking experiences with those who live far away from them. I experienced a very unpleasant situation with someone overseas in my astrology groups. They became aggressive and stalking me. They were reaching out to members of my astrology groups asking questions about me and then e-mailing me through my website very aggressive, threatening e-mails. It was scary. I blocked them on social media but they continued trying to add fake profiles. I also had many people sending me messages that this individual was messaging them asking about my personal life, daughter, husband, and family. For the first time I felt sick to my stomach about helping someone. This person had found my website and e-mailed me through there. They told me all about their eighth house planets and asked me for advice. They said they could not afford a reading but begged for help. I wrote back and offered them to e-mail me three questions and I would give some insight. This person sent their chart and I shared the positive things I saw; they joined my groups. It turned ugly very quickly as they were stalking and messaging strange things in the group and with people offline. They felt like a secret enemy; in my mind at the time it felt that way. They joined other groups and people sent me screen shots of them calling me terrible names and wishing bad things would happen to me. It was shocking, troubling, and made me nauseous. I am more cautious now, and if something feels off, I listen to my intuition. The problem is we often do not see red flags when we are trying to help someone. Sometimes the secret enemies are not real people but sorrow, grief, and loss. Dealing with reality and struggling with stressful practical matters can become our greatest enemy. This can motivate twelfth house people to escape and run away from their problems instead of facing them. Being aware of this energy and how it can manifest in life can help us balance these learning lessons. Even when we encounter secret enemies in life, remember that they are the greatest teachers.

Hidden Talents

One exciting thing about the twelfth house is that it relates to hidden talents. Twelfth house people have special abilities and good luck with certain talents. These talents are often secret and you are not even aware of what they are until something triggers it. For instance, if you have Virgo on the twelfth house you might have a secret talent for writing, communicating and teaching. Leo on the twelfth can create shyness but there can be a special acting talent. Stepping out of your comfort zone can bring unexpected opportunities. The more you do these hobbies, the more opportunities manifest bringing you into alignment with your soul's purpose. If Scorpio is on the twelfth house cusp you might be talented at exposing other people's secrets and excel as a detective, private investigator, or grief counselor. Certain planets placed in the twelfth will also reveal specific talents. The things we are the most uncomfortable with are often associated with our hidden talents. It can be an area of life that feels mysterious and untouchable. Look at the sign or signs that fall on the twelfth, sometimes there is more than one. Analyze the energy of those signs and you can figure out what your hidden talents might be.

Chapter Ten

Depression, Sadness, and Loneliness & Spiritual Connection and Cosmic Consciousness

I remember sitting with a group of friends and feeling totally alone. I felt like I was outside looking in. I never felt supported by those closest to me. I felt sad for most of my life without a reason.
– Anonymous

This prose poem that a friend of mine shared with me, called "Desiderata" by Max Ehrmann from 1927, reminds me of a twelfth house person's struggle with loneliness and their extremely caring and compassionate nature.

Go placidly amid the noise and the haste and remember what peace there may be in silence.
As far as possible, without surrender, be on good terms with all persons. Speak your truth quietly and clearly; and listen to others, even to the dull and the ignorant; they too have their story. Avoid loud and aggressive persons; they are vexatious to the spirit. If you compare yourself with others, you may become vain or bitter, for always there will be greater and lesser persons than yourself. Enjoy your achievements as well as your plans. Keep interested in your own career, however humble; it is a real possession in the changing fortunes of time. Exercise caution in your business affairs, for the world is full of trickery. But let this not blind you to what virtue there is; many persons strive for high ideals, and everywhere life is full of heroism. Be yourself.
Especially do not feign affection. Neither be cynical about love; for in the face of all aridity and disenchantment, it

is as perennial as the grass. Take kindly the counsel of the years, gracefully surrendering the things of youth. Nurture strength of spirit to shield you in sudden misfortune. But do not distress yourself with dark imaginings. Many fears are born of fatigue and loneliness.

Beyond a wholesome discipline, be gentle with yourself. You are a child of the universe no less than the trees and the stars; you have a right to be here. And whether or not it is clear to you, no doubt the universe is unfolding as it should. Therefore, be at peace with God, whatever you conceive Him to be. And whatever your labors and aspirations, in the noisy confusion of life, keep peace in your soul. With all its sham, drudgery and broken dreams, it is still a beautiful world. Be cheerful. Strive to be happy.

Depression is often associated with the twelfth house. Sometimes mental health issues are something that people with twelfth house planets struggle with. Sometimes they can experience depression, anxiety, and sadness due to a highly sensitive nature. Being intuitive, empathic, compassionate, and kind is the main culprit for unpleasant feelings. There is a difference between depression and sadness. Sadness causes feelings of disappointment, loss, sorrow, unhappiness, and can fluctuate. Depression can be a constant circumstance that haunts the daily life. When sadness turns into depression it can be more serious. It might be hard to get out of bed and face the world when you feel depressed. You can't just snap out of depression and sometimes medication and counseling might be needed. Looking at our family history and getting in touch with why you are experiencing these feelings is important. Natural remedies might work in dealing with depressed thoughts. Things like maintaining a healthy diet, sleep routine and doing more exercise can all help produce endorphins in the brain that help reduce depressive symptoms. Sadness can feel different from depression and you can walk through life with sadness and still function normally. There are deeper emotions hiding underneath the surface and they can be disappointment, loss, anger, hurt, and past traumas. Talking to a counselor or friend to process your feelings can be beneficial. It is a strength to ask for help if you are feeling depressed. You do not have to suffer alone; there are many people who will understand. In my twelfth house astrology group, people from all over the world support each other. Many post feelings of loneliness, sadness, and even feelings of suicide. Twelfth house people in the group all weigh in, and offer help and advice because they truly understand. They say the best counselors are people who have survived and experienced the same things as we have. It is hard to listen or respect someone's advice who has not walked in our shoes, or similar shoes at some time. We look for those who understand us.

Twelfth house people often resist getting help for themselves because they are the ones who are always helping others. They are able to listen to others' problems and fully put themselves in their shoes. This is a gift all twelfth house people are born with. Understanding others' pain is enhanced because they are empaths. Listening to others share their feelings about sadness and depression can be cathartic and healing for twelfth house people. This helps them realize they are not alone. There are others out there that experience similar moods. The goal is for twelfth house people to recognize when they need to address these unpleasant feelings. They do not have to live with unhappiness. There are things that can be done to help them feel better. The first step is admitting that they need help and then they need to take steps towards feeling better. Twelfth house people might need more self-care time, relaxation, solitude, affection, or a healthier diet. They do not have to carry the weight of the world on their shoulders. Being a martyr only causes more pain and suffering. Forgiving others is a twelfth house strength but they also need to learn to forgive themselves. They need to be easier on themselves and realize that they do not have to be perfect. They also need to realize that seeking help in any form is a strength.

Spiritual Connection and Cosmic Consciousness

As a twelfth house person, spirituality was something I was naturally interested in. From as long as I can remember, I believed in angels and had a fascination with them. Even though my parents never took me to church, I believed in God. It was an innate feeling that I had within and a sense of knowing that someone was watching over me. Many twelfth house people share with me that they know that there is a purpose to life and a reason they are here. Twelfth house people are born with a spiritual connection to the creative forces. Believing in God or a higher power comes naturally for them and helps encourage them to overcome obstacles. No matter how hard life is twelfth house people are born with faith, belief, and idealism that there is a purpose to the pain they have experienced.

Cosmic consciousness is similar to famous psychologist Carl Jung's theories of the collective unconscious. There is an innate ability in twelfth house people that connects to everyone and everything. A sense of separateness is often felt by people with twelfth house planets, but later in life they realize that they are actually experiencing a "oneness" with others. They realize they are connected to nature and people. Anything in this material world is an illusion, and they realize that there is an energy surrounding and connecting everything. This awareness is part of their mission and learning experience. They have to develop a spiritual path and belief system. Having a spiritual path helps them overcome all of their negative experiences and helps them become more resilient.

Chapter Eleven

Behind the Scenes: Prisons, Hospitals, Monasteries, and Government

Many twelfth house people enjoy being behind the scenes, hiding and keeping their interests private. There is a lot about their personality that no one ever knows. Participating in large groups or social situations makes them feel uncomfortable. They prefer spending time alone to contemplate their thoughts and feelings. They are attracted to career fields that involve helping others that are hidden away. Twelfth house people might be attracted to working in prisons with criminals or in hospitals with those who are mentally ill. The secretive, mysterious, and illusive energy of these places attracts them.

Many people with twelfth house planets are drawn to spiritual work such as serving as priests, nuns, monks, or rabbis. Being able to let go of the self and serve others in a selfless way attracts them. The feeling of being hidden away from the practical world brings peace. I remember in college we had a weekend retreat at a monastery. I stayed the night in one of the rooms where the nuns lived. I felt an enormous connection to the quiet surroundings. I stayed up reading a book and feeling like I was living a past life, it all felt so familiar. Spending time in prayer, meditation, and deep thought contemplating the meaning of life brings comfort. The twelfth house is associated with groups and societies where everyone dresses alike and follows similar rules. I find that many twelfth house people join the military and it relates to foreign travel and that there are rules that everyone follows.

Working with those who have illnesses and suffer with health problems or with individuals struggling with mental illness attract twelfth house people. Volunteering in these types of facilities interests them. When I was in undergraduate school I volunteered in a hospital in St. Louis. I delivered mail all over the hospital to patients and visited people. I remember being on a floor and everyone had liver disease and their skin was yellow. It really bothered me and I realized I could not be happy working in a hospital. I think I have too much Virgo because I have hypochondriac tendencies. People with planets in the twelfth house also have good luck working for the government, and some end up being in positions that bring them out from behind the scenes into the public eye. There are several Presidents who have a twelfth house Sun like Joe Biden, George W. Bush, and Jimmy Carter.

Chapter Twelve

Planets in the Twelfth & Transits through the Twelfth

Sun in the Twelfth

When the Sun is placed in the twelfth house, you are a person who enjoys spending time alone. You like to escape from the world, secluding yourself from the realities of life. You enjoy quiet time and need a peaceful environment to survive. You are extremely sensitive and have a very spiritual nature. You are drawn to anything that is hidden, secretive, and mystical. People who have problems are attracted to you, and helping those who suffer comes easily. You are blessed with psychic abilities and have empathic sensitivity. You feel other people's pain and try hard to help others feel better. Outcasts, abused, and lost souls pull on your heartstrings. It is hard for you to witness anyone suffer, including animals. Working behind the scenes brings peace because you like seclusion and are a very private person. Your emotions are deep and can lead to depression, sadness, and anxiety. Feeling different from others and feeling out of place in large groups is common. You prefer small groups or one on one interaction.

You have a desire to escape from the world and can find yourself on a good path or bad path. The good path for you is when you pursue spirituality, meditation, and dedicate your life to serving others in some way, and the bad path for you is when you turn to alcohol, drugs and other self-defeating behaviors to escape. You are very susceptible to addiction, and need to be cautious about using any types of substances that alter the mind and body. These things can become a crutch used to numb yourself from painful feelings. Learning to be spiritual, having boundaries and helping those in need is your true calling.

You may have father figure issues. When you were younger your father might have been absent or not a strong presence in your daily life. If he was in your life, he might have been emotionally absent. Overcoming feelings of loss, you might unconsciously seek a father figure. Looking up to someone older, attaching to a mentor who serves as a surrogate father figure is common. There can be issues with authority figures and a lack of boundaries between yourself and others. You must put God first in your life and seek a greater spiritual connection to the universe in order to overcome your deep loneliness and sense of separateness. You are truly blessed with extraordinary psychic abilities such as intuition, dreams, and visions, which can be used to help you find a greater purpose in life.

Moon in the Twelfth

When the Moon is placed in the twelfth house, you are a person who has a very sensitive emotional nature. You connect easily to other people's emotions and are deeply spiritual. Your intuition and ability to read other people's intentions is truly a gift. Your emotional nature is often kept secret and hidden from others. Still waters run deep and you often hide your intense emotions from others. Withdrawing on your own and spending time away from the hustle and bustle of the busy world is critical for your emotional balance. Listening to soothing music and surrounding yourself with beautiful art brings peace. Music is very important and brings you comfort in times of stress. You might have artistic talents that you keep hidden because of fears that you are not "good enough". You are hard on yourself and would benefit from learning how to express your intricate emotions through writing, journaling and recording dreams. Your emotional nature is sensitive, and suffering from emotional ups and downs is common. The natural process of emotions such as depression is fascinating to you. You do not necessarily need medication to treat these subdued feelings but would benefit by talking about them, writing about them, or accepting them as a part of life. Sometimes you have a hard time distinguishing your own pain from others' pain.

You feel other people's suffering and absorb that within yourself. You like to run away and hide, but the world needs you. Your spiritual gifts are magnificent and you genuinely care about helping people. You often find yourself drawn to the helping professions caring for the sick, elderly and children. Just make sure you take enough time for yourself and your own inner healing. Self-care is a must with the Moon placed here. The relationship you had with your mother was complex. You might have felt as if you were the "parent" and your mother was the child. Feeling responsible for your mother figure's happiness and always being there when she needed someone to depend on was your role in the family. You may have experienced your mother figure as emotionally vulnerable, weak or unstable. You were the strong one in the relationship and sometimes the caretaker. Your mother may have suffered from depression, grief, trauma or mental illness. This type of parental relationship caused an emotional wound. There could have been intense enmeshment and difficulty separating from the mother figure. If you had to take care of your mother, your emotional needs might have not been met. You learned to do things on your own, making it hard for you to depend on others emotionally. Even though you might have mother figure challenges, you often have an unbreakable bond with your mother and are extremely loyal to her regardless of the situation you had as a child. You can benefit from your mother and may inherit spiritual gifts or abilities from her. She might have been a strong spiritual role model in your life teaching you what was really important versus what was superficial. The relationship often feels karmic, and there are lessons that need to be balanced out between you both.

Venus in the Twelfth

When Venus is placed in the twelfth house, you are a person who hides your romantic feelings and relationships. The twelfth house involves secrets so Venus here has difficulty showing affection and expressing love openly. Suffering can be self-inflicted by making bad decisions and refusing to see things clearly. Deep secrets about your own personality, as well as past lives are locked within you. This placement is an indicator of suffering through love affairs and heartache at some time in your life. The positive energy of this placement is that you are also protected by what seems like a guardian angel watching over you. When you are at your lowest point and almost ready to give up hope, the universe answers your prayers in many ways. You are always protected and guarded more than anyone else by invisible forces. Creative gifts, artistic abilities and talents can be used to create beauty.

You are destined to experience clandestine or secret love affairs. You do not always act on these feelings, they are much more like emotional affairs. Your expression of love is kept secret from others. The initial emotion of love is controlled and sometimes never expressed. You might find yourself in love with someone that is not free or available. You may fall in love with someone who is already married or committed to someone else, or much younger or older than you. I have studied several charts with this placement and often the client reveals to me that they either had an extramarital affair, were in love with someone they could not be with, or they were in love with someone and never told them. Lessons in love are where Venus in the twelfth house people experience the greatest spiritual learning.

Sometimes the feelings are acted on and other times you will keep them hidden and repressed. You may not physically cheat on your partner, but you will have "emotional affairs" because of the energy of this placement. Feelings can overwhelm you and it's difficult for you to let go of those you care about. Even the most moral, committed, and happily married individual can fall prey to this placement. This can be extremely difficult for you, but with understanding and compassion, you will eventually heal. You can suffer as a result of the relationships you find yourself in. It is important for you to truly look within and be honest about your emotions. Attracting partners that have problems, pain or who are different can become a pattern that is difficult to break. You fall in love with people who need your help, share similar wounds and that need someone to take care of them in some way. You can attract unhealthy and abusive partners that might not be mentally stable. You are spiritual and can fall in love easily with other creative, artistic, and spiritual souls. Love and spirituality go hand and hand when Venus is here. Sometimes you can put people up on a pedestal and have illusions about how amazing someone truly is but you only see the good in others. There might be red flags but you can be blinded by love. You have great compassion for those who suffer and are different, loners, misfits, starving artists, and musicians. Sometimes you can get involved in relationships with people who have substance abuse issues such as alcoholism. You are a natural codependent in relationships and need to be careful not to neglect yourself for others. You have to learn to love yourself first before you can truly love others in healthy ways.

This placement blesses the individual with many positive traits such as artistic abilities, creativity, and imagination. You will be able to express your emotions in artistic ways and influence the emotions of others. Creative and imaginative abilities can inspire others and help them see the special gifts of beauty you bring into this world.

You will experience relationships like the ones described above but remember that it is not your fault. Venus here is meant to learn these lessons which show you what it means to find self-love and connection. Learning about this energy can help you approach it in a different way. Being self-aware can help prevent certain situations and relationships from developing. A lot of heartache can be avoided by developing boundaries and realistic expectations of others.

Mars in the Twelfth

When Mars is placed in the twelfth house, you are a person who hides your true feelings and desires. You have a strong spiritual nature and are very intuitive. You are driven and like to delve into the depths of your own mind and the minds of others. Your selfish desires are often hidden from others and no one knows what you really want, including yourself. Sometimes your desires and actions are influenced by a force outside yourself. You often feel an overwhelming sense of mission but avoid opening up to others because of your own unconscious fears.

Struggling with an inability to express your restless nature outwardly and feeling repressed is common. When you feel angry it will be difficult to express it. You tend to turn your anger inward on yourself, which can cause health problems. You should find a healthy outlet to express your energy; exercise, competition, and physical activity every day might help relieve your pent-up energy. You have a strong desire to serve others and help those who are wounded. You can fight for those who are abused, abandoned and alone. You enjoy rescuing people and like to feel that you are appreciated for your kind actions. Your emotions fluctuate between extremes of anger and extreme compassion. Your compassionate nature is intensified with this placement and sometimes you might neglect yourself for others. You will benefit by trying to understand your complex nature by utilizing writing, journaling and spiritual pursuits.

There is a danger for you to become involved with alcohol or other self-destructive behaviors. You need to face your problems head-on and avoid blaming yourself for everything that happens. You may try to escape from painful experiences and find it hard to face daily responsibilities. Living a normal, practical life can feel boring and make you feel trapped. You are prone to depression, which often is a natural part of your personality. You can overcome your loneliness by seeking things that have meaning and finding your own sense of spirituality. You may need to talk to a counselor about your problems and emotions, which will create a healthy outlet for your intense emotions. Hiding your problems from others and being secretive is second nature. When driving or operating machinery you need to be careful. You are vulnerable to cuts and injuries, and may have to have surgery at some time in your life.

Your relationship with your father is something that causes you pain. In childhood, your father might have suffered with alcoholism and was not emotionally or physically there for you. You may have argued with your father and experienced conflict with him. Feeling like there is an absent or missing father figure bond is common. You are on a search for a father figure or someone to look up to. When you turn your energy towards spirituality and connecting with your higher power you will feel more secure. Be careful not to allow your father's problems to become your own. You need to be cautious about using alcohol or drugs, because you are highly susceptible to addiction.

The blessing of this placement is a gift of intense spirituality and compassion. You need to learn to love yourself and open yourself up to others. You will benefit by learning to express yourself freely and trust that others will appreciate your honesty. You will always feel that anger is a difficult emotion to deal with, but the more you embrace it, the more you will grow. You will be happier when you stop allowing others to take your power.

Mercury in the Twelfth

When Mercury is placed in the twelfth house, you are a deep thinker and often hide your true thoughts. You are a person who finds it difficult to express yourself to others. You are shy and can find it difficult to let others into your life because of your private nature. Born with a very perceptive mind, you are a deep thinker who ponders the mysteries of life. You may not always express yourself easily and find it difficult to put words to your emotions. Your intuition and first impressions are likely to be accurate. You are bored with practical learning and enjoy imaginative subjects. When you feel stressed, you enjoy daydreaming and escaping into your imagination. You need time alone to recover from daily life. It is important that you have time to be alone with your thoughts and solitude.

You might have psychic experiences and be able to read others' thoughts. You may have flashes of intuition, and would benefit by writing down your insights. You may enjoy writing and find it easier to jot down your thoughts than say them verbally. Writing can be a great healing resource for you. Your thoughts are so deep it's hard to verbalize them. You can get your thoughts and others' thoughts confused. You are very sensitive to others and the environment you are in. Being able to read people's minds comes easily with practice because of your empathic abilities. You have a spiritual mind and enjoy thinking about the meaning of life and spirituality. You can meditate easily and benefit by quieting your mind. Your mind reaches great depths and you are someone who can be hypnotized easily and are highly suggestible.

Jupiter in the Twelfth

When Jupiter is in the twelfth house, you are a person who is born with intuitive gifts. You are shielded from many of the negative energies of the twelfth house. You have a guardian angel who watches over you, who shields you from the pain and suffering often found here. You have a vivid imagination and optimistic approach to life. You will benefit by doing anything spiritual such as meditation, writing, metaphysics or prayer. You can connect to spirit easily and are blessed with a deep connection to God. You might seek out this relationship by becoming a nun, priest or rabbi. You love to study ancient knowledge and are attracted to things that are deep and meaningful.

You will have good luck coming to you from spiritual work and service to others. The more you serve others, the more blessings will be given to you. You have a strong desire for alone time and solitude. You are highly sensitive in large groups and would prefer to spend time thinking, writing and studying deep subjects. Other people in your life will be drawn to you and will enjoy sharing their problems with you. Your outlook on life is upbeat and optimistic. You are able to answer many questions for others on a variety of spiritual topics. You are born with a natural understanding of life and why we are here. You may have grown up in a family that is very different than you and they will not understand your spiritual nature.

You can sacrifice yourself for a greater spiritual cause and are capable of selfless acts of service. You will receive good luck and blessings each time you make a sacrifice for others. The more you give to others, the more you receive. You attract abundance in many areas and are always searching for a deeper connection to the world. You are someone who enjoys spending time in deep thought and you like to try to figure out what is the purpose of life. You do not enjoy superficial subjects and prefer to live an ascetic lifestyle. You realize that true happiness does not come from the outer world of material possessions, but from within, and by finding your connection to your spiritual source.

You are blessed with psychic gifts and intuitive abilities. You can have visions, impressions and dreams that predict the future. You would benefit by keeping a journal next to your bed at night while you sleep. You need to write your dreams down every night, and it will be beneficial to keep a journal so you can start to write down your intuitive impressions throughout the day. You are luckier than most people who have twelfth house planets and you are shielded from the loneliness that usually comes with the twelfth house.

Saturn in the Twelfth

When Saturn is in the twelfth house, you are a person who tries to repress their fears and doubts. You may suffer from depression and sadness. You will work very hard to cover up your depression and try to overcome it. You need to be easier on yourself and understand that everyone gets depressed, and sometimes feeling sad is normal. Some of the problems occur due to high expectations of yourself and others. You may suffer from guilty feelings and not truly understand where your guilt comes from. You have a fear of the unknown and of being overwhelmed by your emotions. You are a sensitive person and have escapist tendencies. You like to be alone and have time to do things in seclusion. Your emotions are strong and you have to work hard to control them. You spend a lot of time controlling your thoughts, emotions and behaviors.

You may suffer from some type of addiction and you are able to repress the urge for the substance with discipline and willpower. You will have problems with relapse if you do not allow yourself to face the emotions and feelings that led to the addiction in the first place. You do not like to be dependent on others and you avoid sharing your painful feelings with them. You will experience pain and feelings of separateness because you will not allow yourself to open up to others or be vulnerable. You are rigid in your behaviors and will use self-control to overcome many unpleasant emotions.

Even though you do not like relying on others to support you, you enjoy others reaching out to you for help. You are often the person that friends and family turn to for support and understanding. You want to be strong for your family and will set aside your own problems to help them with theirs. Being of service to others will help you break free of your unpleasant guilt and will help you break the chains you impose upon yourself. You need to embrace your psychic abilities and learn how to use them in a practical way.

Uranus in the Twelfth

When Uranus is placed in the twelfth house, you are a person who experiences visions of the future. You are gifted with psychic abilities that seem to come to you instantly. You are a person who needs time to be alone. You are reclusive and enjoy studying mystical subjects behind the scenes. You can experience secret love affairs and fall in love with others easily. You often hide your true feelings for those you care about. You enjoy having freedom to study and time alone to expand your mind.

You need to be careful about abusing substances such as alcohol or cigarettes. You can become addicted to substances easily because you like to experience change and find it exciting. You can suffer from your own instability and rebellious nature. You have an addictive type of personality and can find it difficult to give up things you become obsessed with. Your beliefs about the world are constantly changing. You need to live in an environment that allows you to be free. You have intuitive and psychic abilities that can be used to serve others. You often can see things before they happen and have the gift of clairvoyance.

You need to trust your visions, dreams and perceptions about the future. You would benefit by writing things down and can find that you have a great writing talent. Writing will bring you a sense of peace and will help you balance your restless nature. You need to trust in yourself and allow the universe to send you messages so that you can help uplift others who are suffering. The more you help others who are suffering and allow yourself to change, the more spiritual you will become.

Neptune in the Twelfth

When Neptune is placed in the twelfth house, you are a person who suffers from your own compassionate nature. You are extremely sensitive to the emotions in the environment and to other people. You lack protection from the energetic influences that surround you. You easily pick up what others think, feel and believe. You suffer greatly at times because of your sensitivity. You can feel depressed, withdrawn and sad for no reason. You are a loner and prefer to spend time by yourself. You are imaginative and enjoy thinking deeply about life.

You are a born psychic and are able to understand things about people without them telling you. Absorbing everything in the environment like a psychic sponge you need to learn how to protect yourself and develop stronger boundaries. Others can easily fool you and drain you of your positive energy. You like to believe that everyone is good and spiritual. When you realize the world can be an evil place, you can become despondent. The realization that people can be mean, evil and abusive disturbs you. You prefer to see everyone as loving, kind and compassionate like you are.

You are interested in life after death and hidden realms. You may repress your true emotions and keep them secret from others. You may feel that others will not understand your spiritual beliefs and nature. The older you get, the more spiritual you will become. You need to be careful not to abuse drugs or alcohol because you are highly sensitive to substances that alter the mind. You are prone to addiction and escaping from your emotional pain. You need to face the pain you feel and transform it into a spiritual understanding and bond with God. You are blessed with the ability to connect to God through meditation, prayer and journaling. Your life will be happiest when you follow a spiritual path.

Pluto in the Twelfth

When Pluto is in the twelfth house, you are a person who hides your powerful feelings. You like to hide who you really are. You prefer working behind the scenes and like influencing things secretly. You often have a powerful position and give orders to others behind the scenes. No one will ever truly realize the power you have in the world, because you like to hide the influence you have. You have a very secretive nature and are always hiding emotions from others. You can become obsessed with your romantic feelings and find it hard to concentrate. You can become addicted to your own emotions and develop unhealthy relationships with others that are difficult to end.

You are born with psychic abilities and a deep understanding about life. You are naturally spiritual and seek time alone to meditate, write and think about spiritual issues. You have times when you deny yourself and give up things for your spiritual path. You have intense sexual desires and may try to become celibate as a test to yourself. You like to push the limits and you enjoy feeling the adrenaline of intense emotional interaction. You are a passionate person and enjoy taking risks. You need to be careful about getting involved with drugs or alcohol. You can become addicted easily to substances and find them hard to give up. You bottle up your emotions and keep them secret from others, which can lead to escapism. You feel a powerful need to escape from the world into your imagination or through alcohol. Repressing your anger and rage can make you physically sick. Make sure you learn how to express your powerful emotions in healthy ways.

You will benefit by studying anything spiritual. You need to feel a connection to God and this is where your wound begins. Your relationship with your father was possibly strained or nonexistent. Your father might have had an addiction to alcohol, a mental illness or may have died at a young age. You must learn how to heal and love yourself. You may feel that you do not have a physical father and this causes you immense pain and suffering. You will heal your wound when you learn to turn your face towards God, who is your true father. You are destined to seek a spiritual connection with the universe and this will help you heal your inner wounds.

Chiron in the Twelfth

When Chiron is in the twelfth house, you are a secretive person whose feelings are easily hurt. Deeply empathic, sacrificing your own needs to help others is something that comes naturally. Blindly believing other people and being overly trusting can create emotional wounds. Chiron represents a wound from childhood or a past lifetime. This wound is buried and hidden in the twelfth house. It might take some time for you to feel or understand what your wound is. Something usually triggers this wound whether it be parental divorce, relationship issues, heartbreak or betrayal.

The twelfth house is the area of life that you have the greatest ability to heal your wound. This is the house of everything mystical, angelic and hidden so your wound is often unconscious. It might be later in life when you realize what your wound truly is.

Born with psychic abilities, you are a strong empath and can pick up on the emotions and feelings of others. You might not even realize you are feeling depressed, sad or lonely. Chiron here can cause hurt and deep pain because of a heightened sensitive nature. The world can be cruel and people often let you down which can create a fear about trusting others.

Past life wounds involving spirituality and God are common with this placement. Pain comes from wanting to connect to a spiritual path but sometimes feeling lost or experiencing a blockage from doing so which comes from karmic issues from a previous life. Negative experiences from the past with religion can create a wound surrounding faith.

It is important that you learn to develop strong boundaries to protect your energy from unhealthy people. Those with pain, wounds and suffering will be attracted to you for healing. A deep desire to escape from practical responsibilities can make it difficult to live in the real world. Escaping into your imagination, spending time alone reading and writing can bring comfort. You must face the world, accept the harsh reality that most people are not as kind, caring and forgiving as you are. Overcoming fears surrounding communicating and connecting to God and your spiritual abilities will help you heal your inner wounds.

North Node in the Twelfth (Pisces)

The North Node in your chart represents your soul mission this lifetime.

Virgo is the opposite sign of Pisces and is known as the servant and worker of the zodiac. Virgos tend to worry and over-analyze things. Virgo is service-oriented and enjoys helping others in a practical way. They are analytical and extremely organized. In past lifetimes, as a sixth house South Node person, you mastered the eye for detail and focusing on reality. If North Node is in the twelfth, you have mastered taking care of others in a practical way, possibly even working in the medical field in past lives.

When the South Node is in the sixth, you are learning to move away from controlling traits that no longer are beneficial. The negative personality traits of needing a routine, structure, rules and control need to be released. As a twelfth house North Node person, you are learning to be compassionate and help people in a different way. Learning to have trust and faith in a higher power and in the universe by releasing your need to know everything will help you grow.

In this lifetime, you are now learning to be more Pisces-like, and letting go of your need for perfection is the first step. You might struggle with saying no to others. In this lifetime, twelfth house North Node is learning to let go of guilt and burdens. Learning to let go of any negative emotions that make you feel trapped is critical. You are learning that your own self-worth comes from within by developing a spiritual connection.

You are becoming a twelfth house person and this means that you must learn to be more compassionate with others and yourself. You are learning to release your anxieties and worries. As you move into the Pisces energy, you are going to start feeling more open. Your emotions will start bubbling to the surface. The more you embrace Pisces personality traits, the more you will start feeling things. You will become much more emotional than you were in the past. You will cry easily and more often. This might take some time for you to accept and know that this is a new journey. You will experience new parts of yourself as they emerge. Embrace them, you are learning to be a twelfth house person.

You are learning to move towards a sense of depth of emotion, becoming more deep and more philosophical. The biggest lesson is to learn not to judge yourself or others so harshly. You have high standards for how you expect others to behave. You were a perfectionist, so you know that no one is perfect all the time. You can do your best to try to be perfect, but you are learning to let go of that need. You need to let go of the South Node in sixth house energy. The thing that can help you let go of your need to be perfect is to have trust and faith in a higher power. Your mission with this node is to become spiritual and not resist it. Being practical is something you already mastered; now is the time to be mystical and imaginative. Finding faith in life and seeing things in a more positive light will help you remove critical beliefs.

When you have a twelfth house North Node then you have to put spirituality, God and a spiritual path first. You will benefit by studying psychology, astrology, dreams, meditation and yoga. Immersing yourself in twelfth house hobbies and interests will help you move towards mastering this area of life. You need to pursue activities that will help you connect with your soul and spirit. You are meant to spend time alone and go within yourself to seek answers.

The twelfth house is pulling you to live in the moment and act on feelings. It might not be practical as emotions are not something that can always be controlled. The North Node is always new territory. You are opening up and learning to feel free and comfortable expressing your true nature, and what you really think and feel. Sharing parts of yourself that you have never shared before and letting go of shyness and a cautious nature are great lessons.

North Node in the twelfth will make you a healer and a person who understands what others are going through because you feel it. This node wants you to serve in an emotional, spiritual type of way, and not in the practical basic hands-on way like you did in past lifetimes. Feeling connected to people, by listening to music, can be healing and relaxing. In this lifetime, the twelfth house node is pushing you to develop faith and learn to trust others. You are meant to be intimate and vulnerable with others this lifetime.

You are learning to accept people's flaws without judging them. You are meant to focus instead on believing things are meant to be for a reason. You are learning to develop a connection with God. Balancing your mind, body and spirit will help you heal. When the North Node is in the twelfth, needing time alone will intensify. As you get older, your need to withdraw and escape from the practical side of life will emerge. In your past lives you were used to doing, serving, and working but not comfortable sitting still. You must turn your focus on going within and caring for yourself.

You need to have a good balance and you also have to work to support yourself, but it should not be the focus. The focus is going to change for you as you grow older because when you work you will need it to be meaningful. If you don't find a job that is meaningful to you then you can feel depressed and isolated. People in your life need to realize that as you get older you are going to become more reclusive and withdrawn from the physical world. It does not mean that you will be withdrawn emotionally from your loved ones, but you will need time alone this lifetime to balance your energies. You are meant to let go and surrender to the moment and to your soul mission this lifetime.

Pisces Rising & Sun in the Twelfth

The sign on the twelfth house cusp on the horizon is called the ascendant or rising sign. When Pisces is rising it is a very sensitive placement and makes you like a psychic sponge. Pisces rising makes you a chameleon who can transform and adapt your personality to match other people. Ruled by water and having Neptune energy you are wide open to the energy in your environment. Absorbing stress, happiness, tension, and crisis is often internalized, and it can make you feel depressed and withdrawn. You can put on a happy face when you are around happy people, but if you are surrounded by toxic people, it can have a devastating effect on your health. The rising sign is a mask and Pisces are very good at adapting to whatever environment they are in. You are naturally charming and can pretend to feel, think, and be like others.

You can be experiencing pain but, on the outside, you can fool those closest to you by pretending to be fine. There is a danger of taking on the problems of the world and other people's pain and suffering. When you watch the news or see anything negative or violent, you absorb it and it affects your emotional nature. Symbolized by the fish, you are a fish flapping out in the water. There is no barrier to block out things. Unlike the sign Cancer that has a shell to protect itself and Scorpio, the scorpion that has a sting that can kill, Pisces lacks protection.

A common trait I have seen with Pisces rising is an extremely imaginative and creative personality. Living in a fantasy world and seeing things like you want them to be is Neptune energy manifesting itself. You see people with rose-colored glasses, ignoring all red flags and bad behaviors, sometimes making excuses for others. When in love, you love very deeply. You tend to feel attraction and deep feelings for people who are wounded and attract them. People feel your calming energy and sense that Pisces rising people can heal them just by being in your presence. You often feel like a victim due to how people treat you. You give your trust and open your heart to everyone and can't hide your feelings. When you are upset, frustrated, or angry then people can read it all over your face. Service-oriented and spiritual at heart you express yourself on a higher level than most people. You have difficulty hurting anyone and care about the well-being of others. Feeling needed, wanted, and appreciated is important for Pisces rising individuals. Sadly, feeling taken advantage of and walked on is common. The sad thing is that many people take your kindness as a weakness or take you for granted. It is a shame because in this world true unconditional kindness is rare and it is the Pisces rising individual's greatest strength. They need to remember not to let these negative experiences change who they are, they are truly angels.

You can shut down after you feel hurt or wounded. Feeling depressed and lonely are common feelings you have to learn how to deal with. Sometimes you can feel extreme highs and lows. You just want the pain to go away and want others to treat you with the same kindness in return. The one thing that can help Pisces rising people is seeking a spiritual path. Faith in a higher power and a connection to something outside yourself is important to find. The energy of Neptune helps you connect with the divine and cosmic consciousness through your intuition, imagination, psychic abilities, meditation, writing, and musical abilities. You feel that peace, calmness, and solitude help you heal. You need time to recover and become strong again after stressful situations. Many Pisces rising individuals experience sleep problems due to the influence of the opposite sign, which is Virgo the thinker. Virgos are known as worriers and they dwell, obsess, and overthink everything. Many Pisces rising individuals have those same personality traits in them.

Be careful about who you allow into your inner circle and life because you can attract abusive types of people who want to take advantage. Having the Sun in the twelfth house is similar energy to a Pisces rising personality. Sometimes you feel that others like to take but never give back in return. Loving others unconditionally and with your whole heart is what makes you special. You love in a pure, genuine way and some people can't handle this energy so they push you away. This is when you can start to feel betrayed and abandoned by those you care about. Many people can't handle their own issues because Pisces rising people's kindness and compassion force other people to face their own deep, psychological wounds. They're drawn to Pisces rising for healing, but at the same time they resent them and become uncomfortable with the twelfth house energy. You are meant to serve others, help those who come into your life and then be ready to release them. Those who come to you for healing will not always stay around and Pisces rising people need to avoid blaming themselves for that.

Transits through the Twelfth House

Transit Sun in the Twelfth House

When the Sun transits the twelfth house, there is a strong need for quiet time, solitude, and a need to withdraw from practical responsibilities. You may feel increasingly sensitive and emotional. You will want to escape and isolate yourself more than usual. Issues hidden in your subconscious mind will bubble up and need to be released. This is a good time to let go of old baggage and things you need to get rid of. During this time, you are going to feel drained more than normal and might want to avoid people. Spending time alone now will help you recharge and increase your energy. You feel more compassionate at this time and need more time to rest, sleep, and listen to your intuition.

Transit Moon in the Twelfth House

When the Moon is transiting the twelfth house, your emotions will be heightened. This is a good time to relax and spend time by yourself and take a break from the world. Stay inside and cuddle with your favorite pet, watch old movies, and rejuvenate your energy. Spiritual feelings are intense right now and you might feel a desire to be more connected. Dreams are vivid during this time and it is important to write them down so you can listen to their messages. Do something artistic like singing, writing, drawing, or painting. You may feel a low energy level and experience feelings of depression, guilt, loneliness, and discontent. These feelings will pass. Remember to focus on the positive things in your life during this time.

Transit Mercury in the Twelfth House

When Mercury is transiting the twelfth house you might have difficulties sharing your thoughts and ideas with others. Communication at this time is difficult due to absentmindedness. You will feel more secretive and introverted during this transit. Fears of being misunderstood arise causing conflict with others. You are more inclined to listen but find it hard to communicate during this time and prefer being quiet. Make time to meditate and clear your mind. Journaling and writing your thoughts down on paper might be helpful.

Transit Venus in the Twelfth House

Venus transiting the twelfth house will enhance your need to hide feelings. If you meet anyone new, you are more likely to feel shy and keep your feelings to yourself. If you start a relationship during this transit, you might keep it secret and never tell anyone. This is a positive time in your life and brings happiness to many of your personal relationships. If you are not in a relationship, you might begin a new relationship during this time with someone who you idealize. Be cautious and make sure to take off rose-colored glasses. Strong karmic attractions to people who need help is common. Be careful about getting involved with unhealthy people who tend to take more than they give. Focusing on your spiritual path and letting go of things that are bothering you can be done easily during this transit. This can be a peaceful time where you can get in touch with your creative side.

Transit Mars in the Twelfth House

When Mars transits the twelfth house, your normal drive to achieve things will be dampened. You will want to withdraw, retreat and spend time reflecting on your goals. Other people will drain your energy now so you should try to spend time alone. Imagination is strong with flashes of inspiration, visions and deep dreams that are trying to give you messages. This is a good time to conserve your energy and avoid overworking. Anger can be tested during this time and you might feel things you have not felt before. Allow yourself to feel uncomfortable emotions and avoid escaping from conflict. If you can take some leave and find time to relax, once this transit is over you will be ready to conquer all your goals and obstacles.

Transit Jupiter in the Twelfth House

When Jupiter transits the twelfth house, there is positive energy that can help you give up bad habits you've been struggling with. Eliminating the past and anything that holds you back comes easily during this time. You may become interested in spirituality and mystical subjects. This is a good time to heal the past and to forgive others. Jupiter enhances feelings of generosity and a desire to help others more. Help is given during this transit and you are protected from negative energy and experiences. A desire to travel overseas might happen and inspires you to make travel plans. Take a vacation somewhere near the ocean.

Transit Saturn in the Twelfth House

Saturn transiting the twelfth house brings a heavy, serious energy. You feel more restricted than usual. Repressed memories will come up into conscious awareness for you to heal. If you have a bad habit, it could become unhealthy and destructive during this transit. This is the time to change unhealthy habits. Secrets from the past may weigh you down during this time and it's a good time to talk to someone about what you are going through. This is a time for introspection, and if you have been wanting to go to counseling this is an excellent time to schedule an appointment. Once this transit moves into the first house you will feel a weight lifted off your shoulders.

Transit Uranus in the Twelfth House

When Uranus transits the twelfth house, this will be a time of unexpected change. You will feel more rebellious, eccentric and unconventional. Anything that is traditional will be questioned and your spiritual beliefs will go through a transformation. Secrets will be revealed and parts of yourself that were unconscious will be brought to light. You will change who you are during this transit and once it's over you will realize all the outdated things you left behind. Freedom is an important lesson of this transit and you will need time to pursue things you are interested in. Emotional healing is possible after releasing and letting go of anything that is causing your life to be stagnant. Things will be stripped away during this time but it all happens to create growth.

Transit Neptune in the Twelfth House

When Neptune transits the twelfth house you will feel peaceful and won't mind being alone. Intuition is heightened during this time and you will feel drawn to mystical topics. Experiencing vivid dreams is common during this transit. You will feel extremely emotional and sensitive to other people's energy, thoughts, and pain. Spiritual awakening and transformative experiences can occur, which increase your belief in a higher power. The only downfall is that you might be fooled by others because you will tend to see things with rose-colored glasses during this time. Try to be realistic and see people for how they really are so you avoid being hurt. Try to have realistic expectations and be cautious about taking on other people's problems. Trusting others comes easily during this transit but pay attention to your gut instincts about people and situations.

Transit Pluto in the Twelfth House
When Pluto is transiting the twelfth, things from the past come up for healing. Any unhealed childhood trauma, wounds, relationships issues, or family problems will need to be worked through. Seeing a therapist to process the intense emotions that are affecting you will be beneficial. Transformation of your entire personality, beliefs, and relationships can occur during this transit helping you eliminate old baggage. You might feel more angry, irritable, secretive, and private during this time. There are powerful forces at work in your life. During this transit people will either be drawn to you like a magnet or repelled by your energy. Issues dealing with power and control can manifest in many areas of your life.

Twelfth House Angel Insights
The twelfth house is where you try to escape from the world. It is where you have to learn boundaries and struggle to find self-love. There are often personality traits and things about yourself that are hidden and secret. Illusions also make it difficult to understand your own self and others.

I realized my own planets in the twelfth house showed where my greatest weaknesses and strengths were. I finally recognized the connection between the planet placements in the twelfth as well as the twelfth house transits that I had experienced.

Figuring out what your greatest weakness is comes easily when you look at the planets in your twelfth house. If you don't have planets in the twelfth house, you will want to look at the sign on the cusp of the twelfth.

For instance, if Virgo is on the cusp, you will have a need for perfection, routine, and order. Your greatest weakness could be your own mind, obsessive thoughts, and high standards. You might not realize what your greatest weakness is but you can start looking at the specific planets in the twelfth and what aspects are occurring. Paying more attention to the energies will help you gain deeper self-awareness.

Below you can read stories shared by twelfth house angels about their strengths and weaknesses.

"I have Pluto and Uranus in the twelfth house and my strengths are compassion, intuition, transformation, hidden power, courage, sudden collective visions and psychic awareness. My weakness is pointless rebellion, negative trickster energy, unexpected controversy and powerful enemies."
– S.B.

"As a Sun, Mercury and North Node in the twelfth house person my primary strength is taking the worst situations and learning a lesson from them. Bringing chaos when I am angry is my weakness."
– C.D.

"I have Venus, Mercury and Mars in the twelfth house. My greatest strength is endurance, the ability to suppress pain, such as frustration and anger. Being able to keep going no matter what, even when I am greatly challenged by the people who I thought would never hurt me is my strength. My greatest weakness is forgiving those who betrayed me. My heart is big and it loves

very deeply. Forgiving those who should never have been given the opportunity to be forgiven is what I naturally do. They always seem to keep doing me wrong over and over again."
– M.M.

"My greatest strength and weakness are the same, it's empathy."
– K.M.

"My greatest strength is understanding and my greatest weakness is feeling pain when others are noncommittal in love or when I observe violence."
– F.C.

"Gathering the collective vibration and focusing on twelfth house lessons is my greatest strength. Getting stuck in isolation to prevent being overloaded with energy and escapism is my weakness."
– S.H.

"I have Sun, Venus, Mercury and South Node all in the twelfth house and my greatest strengths are my empathy, compassion, forgiveness, strong mental clarity and intuition. Lacking boundaries, escapism and aloofness are my weaknesses."
– L.B.

"With Mercury and Pluto in the twelfth, my ability to rise to the challenge over and over again is my strength. Fear is my weakness."
– P.C.

"Sun in the twelfth house gives me many strengths such as strong clairsentience, clairvoyance and an innate ability to always be a light through even the darkest of situations, of which I have had far too many since I was very young. My weakness has always been letting people take advantage of my kindness

and willingness to help because I didn't have any boundaries. Empathy is still a weakness."
– R.S.

"I get signs, visions and strength from the divine. I care so much about others that I am blind to the fact that some people do not feel the same way and are not good for my life."
– D.M.

"My greatest strength is isolation and my greatest weakness is letting go."
– C.H.

"With Uranus in the twelfth house, I function best in social isolation and my weakness is an erratic nature."
– P.W.

"Sun in the twelfth house strength is that I am willing to fight tooth and nail against injustices to humans, animals and the environment. My weakness is I keep to myself and not say what I know for fear of ridicule."
– J.W.

"Empathy is both my greatest strength and weakness. I sense everything around me. It's difficult to protect myself from other people's experiences."
– Y.V.

"I have Venus and Pluto in [the] twelfth house. My greatest strength is the ability to connect through writing. Writing helps me feel less alone. My weakness is experiencing terrible anxiety and self-esteem issues and I just want to be comfortable to be myself as fully as I can."
– A.C.

"My greatest strength is understanding the emotions of other people and being very compassionate. My Sun and Venus are in Pisces in the twelfth. My greatest weakness is it is very hard for me to let things go and move on. I also find it difficult to trust my intuition and do not trust it about my own life."
– M.D.

"My Mercury is in the twelfth in Sagittarius and my greatest strength is my sense of humor and ability to tell jokes."
– J.H.

Chapter Thirteen

Twelfth House Angels' Personal Wisdom

Sun, Moon, Mars, Chiron in the Twelfth from J.S., Spain
"As a child, death almost took me three times through drowning. I was adopted at birth from my grandmother because both my parents were drug addicts."

Sun, Venus in the Twelfth from C.T., U.S.A.
"When I was a little girl, I remember feeling other people's pain. I never understood why. I remember riding in the car with my mother when I was five years old. I looked over and saw a homeless man who was limping on the sidewalk. I felt a sadness come over me and I remember asking my mother, 'Mommy, what is wrong with him?' The look on her face showed me that she was uncomfortable with me asking this question. I never forgot what she said, 'He is fine, honey.' It stuck with me, and even at that age, I saw through that answer to the truth. I realized then that I saw things other people did not feel comfortable talking about.

I remember feeling like I was not from Earth. From a young age, I always pondered deep thoughts and felt like I was from another world. I felt different and out of place. I knew I was not from here, and I felt lonely from a young age. Even though I was part of a family, I felt very different from them and even like an outsider looking in at times. I never understood where these feelings came from and what was wrong with me. I had a normal childhood and nothing out of the ordinary. I was born with a vivid imagination and an active dream world. Dreaming has always been a big part of my life ever since I can remember."

Uranus and Pluto in the Twelfth from S.B., U.S.A.
"My experience is that this placement brings considerable insight

into collective dynamics, often in the form of deep intuitions and visions that often arrive in the form of dreams. In a very different sense, my clinical work as a trauma therapist became increasingly effective, resulting in transformative healing for my patients. I've recently embraced writing nonfiction from the perspective of archetypal psychology. My sense is that the suffering of this placement was in some ways karmically necessary and in other ways simply a function of my own struggle to become more conscious and self-aware."

Pluto and Saturn in the Twelfth from L.S., U.S.A.

"Having this combo is like having a police officer and a priest following me around wherever I go. If I step out of line, even a little, I get busted every single time. I can't make it two miles with a headlight out without getting pulled over. I can't lie or it comes back to bite me. I am not allowed to fight back but if I turn the other cheek and allow karma to play out, it does in really mysterious ways. The harder I push for something, the more the universe laughs at me. And then out of nowhere it will provide beyond my wildest expectations. If you tell me no or that I can't do something, get out of my way because I will prove you wrong just for fun. It is equal parts feeling stuck and bursting at the seams. I am gifted but the path is narrow. My life is a beautiful thing. I do everything out of order. I will always get there; I just have to let the universe do its thing."

Saturn, Uranus, Neptune, North Node in the Twelfth from D.T., China

"My mind is dreadful and the call of death always flashes in my mind. I have trouble sleeping and for some reason I have terrible guilt that comes from nowhere. I hold myself to a very high standard and I often judge myself harshly if I feel short of it. I feel the universe is always against me whenever I try my best. There always seems to be obstacles that come from nowhere or a series of backstabbing from my circle of 'friends'. Letting go of expectations about myself, letting go of my need to be perfect and expectations towards others helps me."

Venus in the Twelfth from T.B., U.S.A.

"Venus in the twelfth affected my marriage in many ways and intimacy was nonexistent. I wanted to make art and start selling my creations later in life when I was 50 years old. I had many negative thoughts and had to work hard to overcome them. I am not happy in relationships and have difficulties compromising. I was afraid of being alone and ended up being alone without family. I think my Saturn in the twelfth makes me feel insecure and attracted a husband who was not supportive of my creative pursuits. I need a lot of time alone in seclusion. I follow a spiritual path and that has helped me tremendously. I am still afraid that I will never find true love on a deep level."

Sun, Saturn and North Node in the Twelfth House from D.B., U.S.A.

"For me, twelfth house energy has always made me feel like the wrong one. I have always been criticized. I am always the odd one. I feel like I am ignored until someone wants to criticize me for something. My father was not physically or emotionally abusive, but he could be a jerk and was not attentive. He went to prison for over a decade, and since he has been released, we are on better terms now. He is not a warm person and not affectionate. I have always felt unappreciated in my jobs and my hard work goes unnoticed. I tend to jump from job to job because there is typically a honeymoon period where employers give positive feedback until they forget and start taking me for granted."

Chapter Fourteen

Twelfth House and Self-Care

Twelfth house people benefit by taking time to nurture themselves. Grounding themselves in their physical bodies can be difficult. They benefit by doing activities such as meditation, yoga, walking, reading, and listening to music. Creating art, making pottery, cooking, and writing are all positive ways they can express their emotions. Seeking solitude, alone time, and privacy bring peace and harmony into their lives. Being alone is healing for them, but if they are not able to find enough time to do that, they can become overwhelmed. Stress and anxiety can lead to unhealthy behaviors such as abusing alcohol, food, or other drugs. They want to feel relaxed and seek to find ways to do that even if it's unhealthy. Bad habits and patterns take effort and time to change. With discipline and a goal in mind twelfth house people can change and overcome negative energy. Twelfth house people are connected to the inner spiritual levels and subconscious mind. They are able to tap into energy and replenish themselves naturally if they put positive effort into finding a daily routine. They have talents in manifesting what they want and the universe often provides.

Affirmations

Twelfth house people benefit by practicing affirmations. Affirmations are powerful, positive statements that influence the subconscious mind. Research shows that we think thousands of negative thoughts each day, outweighing positive ones. Shifting our focus on positive affirmations will help us manifest what we want and help us heal. Twelfth house people absorb negative thoughts from others and this can create depression and enhance pessimism.

Some examples of twelfth house affirmations are below:

1. I ask to be shown my part in helping and assisting others.
2. I serve others while having strong boundaries.
3. I unconditionally love myself and others.
4. I take responsibility for my special gifts. I allow myself to trust the conclusion I reach through them.
5. The Universe is friendly towards me. I understand that I am fully loved.
6. My feelings are clear to me. I understand and accept them.
7. My dreams manifest in fulfilling ways.
8. I set practical goals and achieve them.

Meditation and Breathing Exercises

Taking time to still the mind is beneficial for twelfth house people. They are natural at meditation, contemplation, and finding time to be calm. Practicing breathing can also help reduce stress and allow them to connect with their inner emotions. The 12-12-12 breathing exercise is something I was taught in metaphysics school. It will help you get centered and relax your physical body.

12-12-12 Breathing Exercise

1. Sit quietly in a comfortable place.
2. Inhale deeply as you count to 12.
3. Hold your breath for a count of 12.
4. Slowly breathe out for a count of 12.
5. Repeat five times until relaxed.

Yoga and Tai Chi

Twelfth house people benefit from exercise such as walking, yoga, and Tai Chi. Yoga is considered a discipline in India. Yoga balances the mind, body, and spirit. The stretching involved with Yoga helps build muscle strength and flexibility. Yoga can help enhance meditation length and abilities. Tai Chi involves flowing with the movement of energy and connecting to the body. Breathing and movement flowing together help balance energy. Doing yoga and Tai Chi outdoors in nature near water is beneficial for twelfth house people.

Conclusion

The eighth and twelfth astrological houses are special and create transformation in your life. Having planets placed in these houses is a blessing that creates greater resilience, understanding, and spiritual knowledge. My hope is that after reading this book you are not afraid of these houses and can embrace the positive strengths that come through their special life lessons. The world needs deep soul divers to help serve and heal others. You make this world a better place and never forget that you are not alone. There are many other people with similar life experiences, abilities, and feelings. Join other eighth and twelfth house people in my eighth and twelfth house Facebook astrology groups, "The Twelfth Astrological House" and "Deep Soul Divers 8th House Astrology", to connect with other eighth and twelfth house people from all over the world. Thank you for being phoenixes and angels.

O-BOOKS

SPIRITUALITY

O is a symbol of the world, of oneness and unity; this eye represents knowledge and insight. We publish titles on general spirituality and living a spiritual life. We aim to inform and help you on your own journey in this life.
If you have enjoyed this book, why not tell other readers by posting a review on your preferred book site?

Recent bestsellers from O-Books are:

Heart of Tantric Sex
Diana Richardson
Revealing Eastern secrets of deep love and intimacy to Western couples.
Paperback: 978-1-90381-637-0 ebook: 978-1-84694-637-0

Crystal Prescriptions
The A-Z guide to over 1,200 symptoms and their healing crystals
Judy Hall
The first in the popular series of eight books, this handy little guide is packed as tight as a pill-bottle with crystal remedies for ailments.
Paperback: 978-1-90504-740-6 ebook: 978-1-84694-629-5

Your Simple Path
Find Happiness in every step
Ian Tucker
A guide to helping us reconnect with what is really important in our lives.
Paperback: 978-1-78279-349-6 ebook: 978-1-78279-348-9

365 Days of Wisdom
Daily Messages To Inspire You Through The Year
Dadi Janki
Daily messages which cool the mind, warm the heart and guide you along your journey.
Paperback: 978-1-84694-863-3 ebook: 978-1-84694-864-0

Body of Wisdom
Women's Spiritual Power and How it Serves
Hilary Hart
Bringing together the dreams and experiences of women across the world with today's most visionary spiritual teachers.
Paperback: 978-1-78099-696-7 ebook: 978-1-78099-695-0

Dying to Be Free
From Enforced Secrecy to Near Death to True Transformation
Hannah Robinson
After an unexpected accident and near-death experience, Hannah Robinson found herself radically transforming her life, while a remarkable new insight altered her relationship with her father, a practising Catholic priest.
Paperback: 978-1-78535-254-6 ebook: 978-1-78535-255-3

The Ecology of the Soul
A Manual of Peace, Power and Personal Growth for Real People
in the Real World
Aidan Walker
Balance your own inner Ecology of the Soul to regain your
natural state of peace, power and wellbeing.
Paperback: 978-1-78279-850-7 ebook: 978-1-78279-849-1

Not I, Not other than I
The Life and Teachings of Russel Williams
Steve Taylor, Russel Williams
The miraculous life and inspiring teachings of one of the World's
greatest living Sages.
Paperback: 978-1-78279-729-6 ebook: 978-1-78279-728-9

On the Other Side of Love
A woman's unconventional journey towards wisdom
Muriel Maufroy
When life has lost all meaning, what do you do?
Paperback: 978-1-78535-281-2 ebook: 978-1-78535-282-9

Practicing A Course In Miracles
A translation of the Workbook in plain language, with
mentor's notes
Elizabeth A. Cronkhite
The practical second and third volumes of The Plain-Language
A Course In Miracles.
Paperback: 978-1-84694-403-1 ebook: 978-1-78099-072-9

Quantum Bliss
The Quantum Mechanics of Happiness, Abundance, and Health
George S. Mentz
Quantum Bliss is the breakthrough summary of success and spirituality secrets that customers have been waiting for.
Paperback: 978-1-78535-203-4 ebook: 978-1-78535-204-1

The Upside Down Mountain
Mags MacKean
A must-read for anyone weary of chasing success and happiness – one woman's inspirational journey swapping the uphill slog for the downhill slope.
Paperback: 978-1-78535-171-6 ebook: 978-1-78535-172-3

Your Personal Tuning Fork
The Endocrine System
Deborah Bates
Discover your body's health secret, the endocrine system, and 'twang' your way to sustainable health!
Paperback: 978-1-84694-503-8 ebook: 978-1-78099-697-4

Readers of ebooks can buy or view any of these bestsellers by clicking on the live link in the title. Most titles are published in paperback and as an ebook. Paperbacks are available in traditional bookshops. Both print and ebook formats are available online.
Find more titles and sign up to our readers' newsletter at
http://www.johnhuntpublishing.com/mind-body-spirit
Follow us on Facebook at https://www.facebook.com/OBooks/
and Twitter at https://twitter.com/obooks